Rethinking
Anthropology

E. R. LEACH

LONDON SCHOOL OF ECONOMICS
MONOGRAPHS ON SOCIAL ANTHROPOLOGY

Paperback Edition $2.0

RETHINKING ANTHROPOLOGY

LONDON SCHOOL OF ECONOMICS
MONOGRAPHS ON SOCIAL ANTHROPOLOGY

Managing Editor: Anthony Forge

LONDON SCHOOL OF ECONOMICS
MONOGRAPHS ON SOCIAL ANTHROPOLOGY
No. 22

Rethinking
Anthropology

by

E. R. LEACH

HILL
GN6
L434
1966
c.2

UNIVERSITY OF LONDON
THE ATHLONE PRESS
NEW YORK: HUMANITIES PRESS INC.

Published by
THE ATHLONE PRESS
UNIVERSITY OF LONDON
at 2 *Gower Street, London* WC1
Distributed by Constable & Co Ltd
12 *Orange Street, London* WC2

Canada
Oxford University Press
Toronto

First Edition, 1961   *Second impression,* 1963
First Paperback edition with corrections, 1966

Library of Congress Catalog Card No. 66–19115

First printed in 1961 *by*
ROBERT CUNNINGHAM AND SONS LTD
ALVA
Reprinted in 1966 *by photo-litho by*
JOHN DICKENS & CO LTD
NORTHAMPTON

Preface

THE title of this collection properly belongs only to the first essay. On 3 December 1959 I had the honour to deliver the first Malinowski Memorial Lecture at the London School of Economics. The Editorial Board of the London School of Economics Monographs in Social Anthropology generously offered to publish the text of my lecture but added the flattering suggestion that I should reprint a number of my other essays at the same time. I have accordingly appropriated the title of my Malinowski lecture for the whole collection.

The essays extend over a period of fifteen years and I do not pretend that the viewpoint of the latest (Chapter 1) is wholly consistent with that of the earliest (Chapter 2) but there is, I think, a certain continuity of theme and method in all of them. When they were first written all these essays were attempts to 'rethink anthropology'. All are concerned with problems of 'theory' and are based on ethnographic facts recorded by others, my own contribution being primarily that of analyst. In each case I have tried to reassess the known facts in the light of unorthodox assumptions. Such heresy seems to me to have merit for its own sake. Unconventional arguments often turn out to be wrong but provided they provoke discussion they may still have lasting value. By that criterion each of the essays in this book is a possible candidate for attention.

Among social anthropologists the game of building new theories on the ruins of old ones is almost an occupational disease. Contemporary arguments in social anthropology are built out of formulae concocted by Malinowski, Radcliffe-Brown and Lévi-Strauss who in turn were only 'rethinking' Rivers, Durkheim and Mauss, who borrowed from Morgan, McLennan and Robertson-Smith—and so on. Sceptics may think that the total outcome of all this ratiocination adds up to very little; despite all our pedagogical subtleties, the diversities of human custom remain as bewildering as ever. But that we admit. The contemporary social anthropologist is all too well aware that he knows much less than Frazer imagined that he knew for certain. But that perhaps is the point.

The contributions to anthropological pedantry collected in this book add little to the sum of human knowledge but if they provoke some readers to doubt their sense of certainty then they will have served their purpose.

A note on the interconnections between the different papers may prove helpful.

The first draft of Chapter 2 was written in 1943 while I was still on active military service and still in direct contact with Jinghpaw speakers. Although it appeared in the 1945 volume of the *J.R.A.I.* this was not actually published until 1950. These details of dating are relevant because they explain why my paper contains no reference to Chapters 15 and 16 of Lévi-Strauss, *Les structures élémentaires de la parenté* (1949) and reciprocally why the latter work ignores the new information provided by my paper. Chapter 3, which was originally a Curl Prize Essay, was completed in the spring of 1951 and seems to have been the first English language commentary on Lévi-Strauss's *magnum opus* though, presumably, my paper and J. P. B. de Josselin de Jong's monograph *Lévi-Strauss's Theory on Kinship and Marriage* (1952) were going through the press at the same time. Although I here criticized Lévi-Strauss on the grounds of ethnographical inaccuracy my sympathy with his general theoretical point of view is very great. Professor Lévi-Strauss has himself noted the similarity between the view of 'social structure' implicit in my first Jinghpaw paper (Chapter 2) and his own (Lévi-Strauss, 1953, p. 525 n), and in all my subsequent publications my debt to Lévi-Strauss is obvious.

The relationship of Chapter 4 to earlier literature will be apparent from the references in the text. Although it was not intended to be controversial it provoked Dr Kathleen Gough into a vigorous reply (Gough, 1959). The crucial part of my argument here is that I emphasize the need to distinguish between affinity regarded as an alliance between corporate kin groups and those individual affinal ties which bind a particular wife to a particular husband. This theme recurs in Chapter 5 and again in Chapter 1.

Chapter 5, as indicated in the text, is linked with a long correspondence which appeared in the pages of *Man* in 1953 and 1954 but the response which it evoked from my close academic colleagues is only marginally connected with this earlier discussion. Dr Goody has denounced my whole argument as grounded in fundamental error (Goody, 1959, p. 86) and Professor Fortes has taken up most of two issues of *Man* to expound my fallacies and confusions (Fortes, 1959b). Both these explosions of academic wrath were provoked by a single sentence in my essay, namely —'Thus Fortes, while recognizing that ties of affinity have comparable importance to ties of descent, disguises the former under his expression "complementary filiation" ' (see below p. 122). The exact sense in which this statement is an 'error' is still not clear to me for in the course of his denunciation Fortes reaffirms his view that 'complementary filiation is a function of affinal relations' (Fortes, 1959b, p. 209) which is precisely the argument I sought to controvert.

Professor Fortes has called his article 'a rejoinder to Leach', and readers of Chapter 1 of this book need to appreciate that among other things it is intended as 'a rejoinder to Fortes'. Reference to a short note in *Man* (1960, Art. 6) will perhaps help to make this clear.

The two short papers on time symbolism reprinted in Chapter 6 do not form a series with the other chapters of the book though again the influence of Professor Lévi-Strauss is pronounced. Although my 'Cronus and Chronos' appeared in print in 1953 while Lévi-Strauss's 'The Structural Study of Myth' was only published in 1956, I had in fact already heard Professor Lévi-Strauss's lecture on this topic before I wrote my essay. *Explorations*, the Toronto University publication in which my Chapter 6 was originally published, carried on its fly leaf the statement that it was 'designed, not as a permanent reference journal that embalms truth for posterity, but as a publication that explores and searches and questions' and both my papers are correspondingly brief and tentative. Nevertheless a number of my friends have suggested that the arguments they contain are of more than ephemeral interest; hence the reissue here.

Chapter 1 contains a considerable amount of matter which was not included in the spoken text of my Malinowski lecture. The other essays appear as originally printed, except for the correction of misprints, and one or two very minor alterations intended to clarify the argument. The Introductory Notes at the beginning of Chapters 2–6 are new.

Acknowledgements: I am indebted to the Council of the Royal Anthropological Institute of Great Britain and Ireland for permission to reprint the essays published here as Chapters 2, 3, 4 and 5 and to Professor E. S. Carpenter and the University of Toronto for permission to reprint the two short essays included in Chapter 6.

I am indebted to a personal grant in aid from the Behavioral Sciences Division of the Ford Foundation for facilities employed while preparing these papers for publication.

E. R. L.

Contents

I

Rethinking Anthropology

LET me begin by explaining my arrogant title. Since 1930 British Social Anthropology has embodied a well defined set of ideas and objectives which derive directly from the teaching of Malinowski and Radcliffe-Brown—this unity of aim is summed up in the statement that British social anthropology is *functionalist* and concerned with *the comparative analysis of social structures*. But during the last year or so it has begun to look as if this particular aim had worked itself out. Most of my colleagues are giving up the attempt to make comparative generalizations; instead they have begun to write impeccably detailed historical ethnographies of particular peoples.

I regret this new tendency for I still believe that the findings of anthropologists have general as well as particular implications, but why has the functionalist doctrine ceased to carry conviction? To understand what is happening in social anthropology I believe we need to go right back to the beginning and *rethink* basic issues—really elementary matters such as what we mean by marriage or descent or the unity of siblings, and that is difficult—for basic concepts are basic; the ideas one has about them are deeply entrenched and firmly held.

One of the things we need to recognize is the strength of the empirical bias which Malinowski introduced into social anthropology and which has stayed with us ever since. The essential core of social anthropology is fieldwork—the understanding of the way of life of a single particular people. This fieldwork is an extremely personal traumatic kind of experience and the personal involvement of the anthropologist in his work is reflected in what he produces.

When we read Malinowski we get the impression that he is stating something which is of *general* importance. Yet how can this be? He is simply writing about Trobriand Islanders. Somehow he has so assimilated himself into the Trobriand situation that he is able to make the Trobriands a microcosm of the whole primitive world. And the same is true of his successors; for Firth, Primitive Man is a Tikopian, for Fortes, he is a citizen of Ghana. The existence of this prejudice has long been recognized but we have paid inadequate attention to its consequences. The difficulty of achieving comparative generalizations is directly linked with the problem of escaping from ethnocentric bias.

As is appropriate to an occasion when we honour the memory of Bronislaw Malinowski, I am going to be thoroughly egotistical. I shall imply my own merit by condemning the work of my closest friends. But there is method in my malice. My purpose is to distinguish between two rather similar varieties of comparative generalization, both of which turn up from time to time in contemporary British social anthropology. One of these, which I dislike, derives from the work of Radcliffe-Brown; the other, which I admire, derives from the work of Lévi-Strauss. It is important that the differences between these two approaches be properly understood, so I shall draw my illustrations in sharp contrast, all black and all white. In this harsh and exaggerated form Professor Lévi-Strauss might well repudiate the authorship of the ideas which I am trying to convey. Hence my egotism; let the blame be wholly mine.

My problem is simple. How can a modern social anthropologist, with all the work of Malinowski and Radcliffe-Brown and their successors at his elbow, embark upon generalization with any hope of arriving at a satisfying conclusion? My answer is quite simple too; it is this: *By thinking of the organizational ideas that are present in any society as constituting a mathematical pattern.*

The rest of what I have to say is simply an elaboration of this cryptic statement.

First let me emphasize that my concern is with *generalization*, not with *comparison*. Radcliffe-Brown maintained that the objective of social anthropology was the 'comparison of social structures'. In explaining this he asserted that when we distinguish and compare different types of social structure we are doing the same kind of thing as when we distinguish different kinds of sea shell according to their structural type (Radcliffe-Brown, 1953, p. 109). *Generalization* is quite a different kind of mental operation.

Let me illustrate this point.

Any *two* points can be joined by a straight line and you can represent this straight line mathematically by a simple *first* order algebraic equation.

Any *three* points can be joined by a circle and you can represent this circle by a quadratic or *second* order algebraic equation.

It would be a *generalization* to go straight on from there and say: any n points in a plane can be joined by a curve which can be represented by an equation of order n-1. This would be just a guess, but it would be true, and it is a kind of truth which no amount of comparison can ever reveal.

Comparison and generalization are both forms of scientific activity, but different.

Comparison is a matter of butterfly collecting—of classification, of the arrangement of things according to their types and subtypes. The followers of Radcliffe-Brown are anthropological butterfly collectors and their approach to their data has certain consequences. For example, according to Radcliffe-Brown's principles we ought to think of Trobriand society as a society of a particular structural type. The classification might proceed thus:

Main Type:	societies composed of unilineal descent groups.
Sub-type:	societies composed of matrilineal descent groups.
Sub-sub-type:	societies composed of matrilineal descent groups in which the married males of the matrilineage live together in one place and apart from the females of the matrilineage,

and so on.

In this procedure each class is a sub-type of the class immediately preceding it in the tabulation.

Now I agree that analysis of this kind has its uses, but it has very serious limitations. One major defect is that it has no logical limits. Ultimately every known society can be discriminated in this way as a sub-type distinct from any other, and since anthropologists are notably vague about just what they mean by 'a society', this will lead them to distinguish more and more societies, almost *ad infinitum*.

This is not just hypothesis. My colleague Dr Goody has gone to great pains to distinguish *as types* two adjacent societies in the Northern Gold Coast which he calls LoWiili and LoDagaba. A careful reader of Dr Goody's works will discover, however, that these two 'societies' are simply the way that Dr Goody has chosen to describe the fact that his field notes from two neighbouring communities show some curious discrepancies. If Dr Goody's methods of analysis were pushed to the limit we should be able to show that every village community throughout the world constitutes a distinct society which is distinguishable as a type from any other (Goody, 1956b).

Another serious objection is that the typology makers never explain why they choose one frame of reference rather than another. Radcliffe-Brown's instructions were simply that 'it is necessary to compare societies with reference to one particular aspect . . . the economic system, the political system, or the kinship system' . . . this is equivalent to saying that you can arrange your butterflies according to their colour, or their size, or the shape of their wings according to the whim of the moment, but no matter what you do this will be science. Well perhaps, in a sense, it is; but you must realize that your prior arrangement creates an initial bias from which it is later extremely difficult to escape (Radcliffe-Brown, 1940, p. xii).

Social anthropology is packed with frustrations of this kind. An obvious example is the category opposition patrilineal/matrilineal. Ever since Morgan began writing of the Iroquois, it has been customary for anthropologists to distinguish unilineal from non-unilineal descent systems, and among the former to distinguish patrilineal societies from matrilineal societies. These categories now seem to us so rudimentary and obvious that it is extremely difficult to break out of the straitjacket of thought which the categories themselves impose.

Yet if our approach is to be genuinely unbiased we must be prepared to consider the possibility that these type categories have no sociological significance whatsoever. It *may* be that to create a class labelled *matrilineal societies* is as irrelevant for our understanding of social structure as the creation of a class *blue butterflies* is irrelevant for the understanding of the anatomical structure of L-pidoptera. I don't say it is so, but it may be; it is time that we considered the possibility.

But I warn you, the rethinking of basic category assumptions can be very disconcerting.

Let me cite a case. Dr Audrey Richards's well-known contribution to *African Systems of Kinship and Marriage* is an essay in Radcliffe-Brownian typology making which is rightly regarded as one of the 'musts' of undergraduate reading (Richards, 1950).

In this essay Dr Richards asserts that '*the* problem' of matrilineal societies is the difficulty of combining recognition of descent through the woman with the rule of exogamous marriage, and she classifies a variety of matrilineal societies according to the way this 'problem' is solved. In effect her classification turns on the fact that a woman's brother and a woman's husband jointly possess rights in the woman's children but that matrilineal systems differ in the way these rights are allocated between the two men.

What I object to in this is the prior category assumptions. Men have brothers-in-law in all kinds of society, so why should it be assumed from the start that brothers-in-law in matrilineal societies have special 'problems' which are absent in patrilineal or bilateral structures? What has really happened here is that, because Dr Richards's own special knowledge lay with the Bemba, a matrilineal society, she has decided to restrict her comparative observations to matrilineal systems. Then, having selected a group of societies which have nothing in common except that they are matrilineal, she is naturally led to conclude that matrilineal descent is *the* major factor to which all the other items of cultural behaviour which she describes are functionally adjusted.

Her argument I am afraid is a tautology; her system of classification already implies the truth of what she claims to be demonstrating.

This illustrates how Radcliffe-Brown's taxonomic assumptions fit in with the ethnocentric bias which I mentioned earlier. Because the type-finding social anthropologist conducts his whole argument in terms of particular instances rather than of generalized patterns, he is constantly tempted to attach exaggerated significance to those features of social organization which happen to be prominent in the societies of which he himself has first hand experience.

The case of Professor Fortes illustrates this same point in rather a different way. His quest is not so much for types as for prototypes. It so happens that the two societies of which he has made a close study have certain similarities of structural pattern for, while the Tallensi are patri-

RETHINKING ANTHROPOLOGY 5

lineal and the Ashanti matrilineal, both Tallensi and Ashanti come un-
usually close to having a system of double unilineal descent.

Professor Fortes has devised a special concept, 'complementary filiation',
which helps him to describe this double unilineal element in the Tallensi/
Ashanti pattern while rejecting the notion that these societies actually
possess double unilineal systems (Fortes, 1953, p. 33; 1959b).

It is interesting to note the circumstances which led to the development
of this concept. From one point of view 'complementary filiation' is
simply an inverse form of Malinowski's notion of 'sociological paternity'
as applied in the matrilineal context of Trobriand society. But Fortes has
done more than invent a new name for an old idea; he has made it the
corner stone of a substantial body of theory and this theory arises logically
from the special circumstances of his own field experience.

In his earlier writings the Tallensi are often represented as having a
somewhat extreme form of patrilineal ideology. Later, in contrast to
Rattray, Fortes placed an unambiguously matrilineal label upon the
Ashanti. The merit of 'complementary filiation', from Fortes's point of
view, is that it is a concept which applies equally well to both of these
contrasted societies but does not conflict with his thesis that both the
Tallensi and the Ashanti have systems of unilineal descent. The concept
became necessary to him precisely because he had decided at the start
that the more familiar and more obvious notion of double unilineal
descent was inappropriate. In retrospect Fortes seems to have decided
that double unilineal descent is a special development of 'complementary
filiation', the latter being a feature of all unilineal descent structures. That
such category distinctions are contrived rather than natural is evident
from Goody's additional discrimination. Goody asserts that the LoWiili
have 'complementary descent rather than a dual descent system'. Since
the concept of 'complementary filiation' was first introduced so as to help
in the distinction between 'filiation' and 'descent' and since the adjective
'complementary' cannot here be given meaning except by reference to the
word 'descent', the total argument is clearly tautologous (Fortes, 1945,
pp. 134, 200f; 1950, p. 287; 1953, p. 34; 1959; Goody, 1956b, p. 77).

Now I do not claim that Professor Fortes is mistaken, but I think he is
misled by his prior suppositions. If we are to escape both from typology
making and from enthnocentric bias we must turn to a different kind of
science. Instead of comparison let us have generalization; instead of
butterfly collecting let us have inspired guesswork.

Let me repeat. Generalization is inductive; it consists in perceiving
possible general laws in the circumstances of special cases; it is guesswork,
a gamble, you may be wrong or you may be right, but if you happen to
be right you have learnt something altogether new.

In contrast, arranging butterflies according to their types and sub-types
is tautology. It merely reasserts something you know already in a slightly
different form.

But if you are going to start guessing, you need to know *how* to guess. And this is what I am getting at when I say that the form of thinking should be mathematical.

Functionalism *in a mathematical* sense is *not* concerned with the inter-connections between parts of a whole but with the principles of operation of partial systems.

There is a direct conflict here with the dogmas of Malinowski and Radcliffe-Brown. Malinowski's functionalism required us to think of each Society (or Culture, as Malinowski would have put it) as a totality made up of a number of discrete empirical 'things', of rather diverse kinds—e.g. groups of people, 'institutions', customs. These 'things' are functionally interconnected to form a delicately balanced mechanism rather like the various parts of a wrist watch. The functionalism of Rad-cliffe-Brown was equally mechanical though the focus of interest was different.

Radcliffe-Brown was concerned, as it were, to distinguish wrist watches from grandfather clocks, whereas Malinowski was interested in the general attributes of clockwork. But *both* masters took as their starting point the notion that a culture or a society is an empirical whole made up of a limited number of readily identifiable parts and that when we compare two societies we are concerned to see whether or not the same kinds of parts are present in both cases.

This approach is appropriate for a zoologist or for a botanist or for a mechanic but it is *not* the approach of a mathematician nor of an engineer and, in my view, the anthropologist has much in common with the en-gineer. But that is *my* private bias. I was originally trained as an engineer.

The entities which we call societies are not naturally existing species, neither are they man-made mechanisms. But the analogy of a mechanism has quite as much relevance as the analogy of an organism.

This is not the place to discuss the history of the organic analogy as a model for Society, but its arbitrariness is often forgotten. Hobbes, who developed his notion of a social organism in a very systematic way, dis-cusses in his preface whether a mechanical or an organic analogy might be the more appropriate for his purpose. He opts for an organism only because he wants to include in his model a metaphysical prime mover (i.e. God—Life Force) (Hobbes, 1957, p. 5). In contrast Radcliffe-Brown employed the organic analogy as a matter of dogma rather than of choice (e.g. Radcliffe-Brown, 1957, pp. 82–86; 1940a, pp. 3, 10) and his butterfly collecting followers have accepted the appropriateness of the phrase 'social organism' without serious discussion. Against this complacency I must protest. It is certainly the case that social scientists must often resort to analogy but we are not committed to one type of model making for all eternity.

Our task is to understand and explain what goes on in society, how societies work. If an engineer tries to explain to you how a digital computer works he doesn't spend his time classifying different kinds of nuts and bolts. He concerns himself with principles, not with things. He writes out his argument as a mathematical equation of the utmost simplicity, somewhat on the lines of: $0 + 1 = 1$; $1 + 1 = 10$.

No doubt this example is frivolous; such computers embody their information in a code which is transmitted in positive and negative impulses denoted by the digital symbols 0 and 1. The essential point is that although the information which can be embodied in such codes may be enormously complex, the basic principles on which the computing machines work is very simple. Likewise I would maintain that quite simple mechanical models can have relevance for social anthropology despite the acknowledged fact that the detailed empirical facts of social life display the utmost complexity.

I don't want to turn anthropology into a branch of mathematics but I believe we can learn a lot by starting to think about society in a mathematical way.

Considered mathematically society is not an assemblage of things but an assemblage of variables. A good analogy would be with that branch of mathematics known as topology, which may crudely be described as the geometry of elastic rubber sheeting.

If I have a piece of rubber sheet and draw a series of lines on it to symbolize the functional interconnections of some set of social phenomena and I then start stretching the rubber about, I can change the manifest shape of my original geometrical figure out of all recognition and yet clearly there is a sense in which it is the *same* figure all the time. The constancy of pattern is not manifest as an objective empirical fact but it is there as a mathematical generalization. By analogy, generalized structural patterns in anthropology are not restricted to societies of any one manifest structural type.

Now I know that a lot of you will tell me that topology is one of those alarming scientific mysteries which mere sociologists had best avoid, but I am not in fact proposing anything original. A very good simple account of the nature of *topology* appears in an article under that title in the current edition of the *Encyclopaedia Britannica*. The author himself makes the point that because topology is a non-metrical form of mathematics it deserves especial attention from social scientists.

The fundamental variable in topology is the degree of connectedness. Any closed curve is 'the same as' any other regardless of its shape; the arc of a circle is 'the same as' a straight line because each is open ended. Contrariwise, a closed curve has a greater degree of connectedness than an arc. If we apply these ideas to sociology we cease to be interested in particular relationships and concern ourselves instead with the regularities of pattern among neighbouring relationships. In the simplest possible case if there be a relationship p which is intimately associated with another relationship q then in a topological study we shall not concern ourselves

with the particular characteristics of p and q but with their mutual characteristics, i.e. with the algebraic ratio p/q. But it must be understood that
the relationships and sets of relationships which are symbolized in this
way cannot properly be given specific numerical values. The reader
should bear this point in mind when he encounters the specimens of
pseudo-mathematics which occur later in this paper.

All propositions in topology can also be expressed as propositions in
symbolic logic (see Carnap, 1958, chapter G) and it was probably a
consideration of this fact which led Nadel to introduce symbolic logic into
his last book (Nadel, 1957). My own view is that while the consideration
of mathematical and logical models may help the anthropologist to order
his theoretical arguments in an intelligent way, his actual procedure
should be non-mathematical.

The relevance of all this to my main theme is that the *same* structural
pattern may turn up in *any* kind of society—a mathematical approach
makes no prior assumption that unilineal systems are basically different
from non-unilineal systems or patrilineal structures from matrilineal
structures. On the contrary, the principle of parity leads us to discount
all rigid category distinctions of this kind.

Let me try to illustrate my point with an example. To be appropriate
for the occasion I shall take my example from Malinowski.

Most of you will know that Malinowski reported, as a fact of empirical
ethnography, that the Trobrianders profess ignorance of the connection
between copulation and pregnancy and that this ignorance serves as a
rational justification for their system of matrilineal descent. From the
Trobriand point of view 'my father' (*tama*) is not a blood relative at all
but a kind of affine, 'my mother's husband' (Malinowski, 1932a, p. 5).

However, alongside their dogmatic ignorance of the facts of life,
Trobrianders also maintain that every child should resemble its mother's
husband (i.e. its father) but that no child could ever resemble a member
of its own matrilineal kin.

Malinowski seems to have thought it paradoxical that Trobrianders
should hold both these doctrines at the same time. He was apparently
bemused by the same kind of ethnocentric assumptions as later led a
Tallensi informant to tell Professor Fortes that 'both parents transmit their
blood to their offspring, *as can be seen from the fact* that Tallensi children
may resemble either parent in looks' (Fortes, 1949, p. 35; my italics).
This is mixing up sociology and genetics. We *know*, and apparently the
Tallensi assume, that physical appearance is genetically based, but there
is no reason why primitive people in general should associate ideas of
genetic inheritance with ideas about physical resemblance between
persons. The explanation which the Trobrianders gave to Malinowski
was that a father impresses his appearance on his son by cohabiting
repeatedly with the mother and thereby 'moulding' (*kuli*) the child in her
womb (Malinowski, 1932a, p. 176) which is reminiscent of the Ashanti

view that the father shapes the body of his child as might a potter (Rattray, 1929, p. 9). This Trobriand theory is quite consistent with the view that the father is related to the son only as mother's husband—that is, an affine and not as a kinsman.

There are other Trobriand doctrines which fall into line with this. The father's sister is 'the prototype of the lawful woman' (Malinowski, 1932a, p. 450) which seems to be more or less the equivalent of saying that the father (*tama*) is much the same sort of relation as a brother-in-law. Again, although, as Powell has shown (Powell, 1956, p. 314), marriage with the father's sister's daughter is rare, the Trobrianders constantly assured Malinowski that this was a very right and proper marriage. Evidently in their view the category *tama* (which includes both father and father's sister's son) is very close to that of *lubou* (brother-in-law) (Malinowski, 1932a, pp. 86, 451). The similarity is asserted not only in verbal expression but also in the pattern of economic obligation, for the harvest gift (*urigubu*) paid by a married man is due *both* to his mother's husband (*tama*) *and* to his sister's husband (*lubou*) (Malinowski, 1935, I, pp. 386, 413–18).

From my point of view this cluster of Trobriand beliefs and attitudes is a 'pattern of organizational ideas'—it specifies a series of categories, and places them in a particular relationship with one another as in an algebraic equation. But Malinowski was biased by his down to earth empiricism, by European prejudices and by his interest in psycho-analysis, and he refused to accept the Trobriand doctrine at its face value. Instead he refurbished his concept of 'sociological paternity' which he had originally devised to fit a quite different context, that of patrilineal organization among the Australian Aborigines (Malinowski, 1913, p. 170–83).

On this earlier occasion Malinowski had used 'sociological paternity' to show how relations between parents and children and between spouses derive from customary rules and not from any universal facts of biology or psychology, but in the later application of these ideas to Trobriand circumstances he shifts his ground and the argument becomes confused by the introduction of naive psychological considerations.

On the face of it 'sociological paternity', as used in *The Sexual Life of Savages*, seems to mean that even in a society which, like the Trobriands, denies the facts of 'biological paternity', sociological attitudes which pertain to paternity, as *we* understand it, may still be found. So far, so good. But Malinowski goes further than this. Instead of arguing, as in the Australian case, that kinship attitudes have a purely social origin, he now insists that social attitudes to kinship are rooted in universal psychological facts. The paternal relationship contains elements which are necessarily present in the father/child relationship of *all* societies, no matter what the circumstances of custom and social structure may be. This is all very confusing. On the one hand the reader is told quite plainly that the Trobriand child is taught to think of his father as a non-relative, as an individual with the special non-kinship status of mother's husband. But on the other hand the reader is forced to conclude that this Trobriand mother's husband is related to the mother's child 'as a sociological father', that is to say by ties of kinship as well as by ties of affinity. The argument, as a whole, is self-contradictory.

You may well think that this is a very hairsplitting point to make a fuss about. How can it possibly make any difference whether I think of a particular male as my father or as my mother's husband?

Well, all I can say is that anthropologists do worry about such things. Professor Fortes, Dr Goody and Dr Kathleen Gough are so disturbed by my heretical views on this subject that each of them has recently taken time off to try to bruise my head with their private recensions of Malinowski's argument (Fortes, 1959b; Goody, 1959, pp. 83, 86; Gough, 1959).

The heart of the controversy may be stated thus. To Englishmen it seems obvious that the relation between brothers-in-law is radically different from the relation between father and son. By that we mean that the rights and duties involved in the two cases are quite different *in kind*. The first relation is one of affinity; the second is one of filiation.

It also seems obvious to us that the relation between mother and son, though different from the relation between father and son, is nevertheless of the same general kind—it is again a relation of filiation. Now Fortes and his followers maintain that this is universally the case—that the relations between a child and *either* of its parents are of the same basic kind, relations of filiation. Fortes asserts that it is necessary to maintain this because any other view 'would make the incest taboo nonsensical'. Thus, like Malinowski, he is prepared on dogmatic psychological grounds to repudiate the Trobrianders' views of their own social system (Fortes, 1959b, p. 194).

The contrary approach, which is my heresy, is that we must take each case as it comes. If the Trobrianders say—as they do say both in word and deed—that the relation between a father and his son is much the same as the relation between male cross-cousins and as the relation between brothers-in-law, but absolutely different from the relation between a mother and her child, then we must accept the fact that this is so. And in that case we only delude ourselves and everyone else if we call such a relationship *filiation*.

My disagreement with Professor Fortes on this matter turns on this point. It seems to me that in his use of the term 'complementary filiation' he is trying to establish as a universal a special ethnographic phenomenon which he happens to have observed among the Tallensi and the Ashanti.

For my part I have no anxiety to demonstrate anything. I am interested only in discerning *possible* general patterns in the peculiar facts of particular ethnographies.

Let us see if we can examine this issue, not as a problem of comparative social structure, nor of verbal polemic, but as a case of generalized (mathematical) structural pattern.

The cardinal principle of Malinowski's anthropological method was that we should view the system as a whole and examine the interconnections between the parts. Thus, in his view, all the following Trobriand facts are closely interconnected:

1. A father is deemed to have no biological connection with his child.
2. A child shares the blood of its mother and her siblings; a father is related to his child as 'mother's husband'.
3. Marriage is virilocal; a boy at marriage sets up house in the hamlet of his mother's brother and his wife joins him there. After marriage brothers and sisters live in different hamlets. They must avoid one another.
4. An individual's own 'blood relatives'—his matrilineal kin—are never suspected of sorcery or witchcraft; affinal relatives, including wives and children, are often so suspected.
5. Children are thought to resemble their fathers but not their mothers.
6. During a man's lifetime his wife's brother gives him an annual gift of food.
7. At his death his lineage kinsmen make large payments to his wife's lineage. All activities connected with the disposal of the corpse are carried out by members of the wife's lineage.

The list of relevant interconnected facts could be extended indefinitely, but these are the items to which Malinowski himself seems to have attached most weight (see Fig. 1).

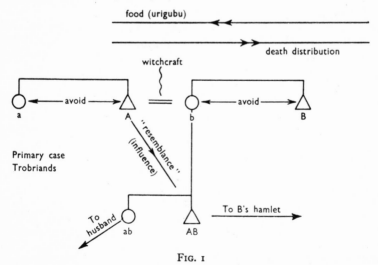

FIG. 1

All of us now accept this principle of the functional interconnection of items of cultural behaviour, but *generalization* calls for an exactly opposite treatment of the data. If we are to generalize, a small cluster of interconnected facts must be treated as an isolate expressing a particular principle of social mechanism.

Now consider Fig. 2 and regard it as a generalized version of the centre of Fig. 1. I want to consider the relations of filiation *not* in relation to the system as a whole but in relation to one another.

In talking about 'function' in a *generalized* way it is not sufficient to specify relationship between particular empirical facts; we must give a genuine mathematical sense to our concept of function and start thinking in terms of ratios and the variations of ratios.

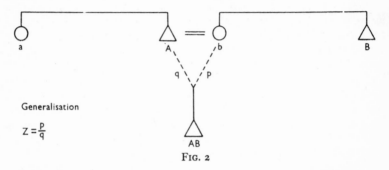

Generalisation

$$Z = \frac{p}{q}$$

Fig. 2

So now please forget about my list of cultural characteristics and turn your attention to the diagram (Fig. 2). Try to think of this as a mathematical expression and forget for the moment that it was originally derived from Trobriand ethnography. I want to 'generalize' this pattern. Instead of using a value loaded term like *filiation* we will use algebra. Filiation with the father $= 'q'$, filiation with the mother $= 'p'$.

The ratio p/q is a mathematical function which varies along with variations of 'p' and 'q'. As indicated above I want to think of these items as topological variables rather than as measurable quantities.

If we call this function z it is clear that z has an infinite number of values between o and infinity. The Trobriand case evidently represents one extreme:

$$q = \text{o}; \ p = 1; \ z = \text{infinity}$$

The opposite extreme would be:

$$p = \text{o}; \ q = 1; \ z = \text{o}$$

And there is also an interesting special case somewhere in the middle:

$$q = p; \ z = 1$$

In the great majority of cases we must expect both 'p' and 'q' to have values but the exceptional cases where either 'p' or 'q' is zero are clearly of great interest.

I am *not* trying to argue that we can use mathematics to solve anthropological problems. What I do claim is that the abstraction of mathematical statement has great virtues in itself. By translating anthropological facts into mathematical language, however crude, we can get away from excessive entanglement in empirical facts and value loaded concepts.

When mathematicians write down equations it doesn't worry them overmuch whether any particular instance is going to turn out 'real' or 'imaginary', but I am prepared to admit that the only kinds of structural pattern which interest anthropologists are those which actually occur.

Well, do my equations represent real or imaginary situations?

For example, what about $z = 0$; $q = 1$; $p = 0$? Obviously an impossible case, for this would imply a society in which a child is not related to its mother, which is absurd. But wait a minute. Why is it absurd? Why is it more absurd than Malinowski's case where a child in unrelated to its father? Mathematically speaking the two cases are precisely on a par; the virtue of mathematical statement is that it allows us to see at once the similarities of pattern in this sense.

Now the Malinowski of *The Family among the Australian Aborigines* would have accepted this equivalence for he argued quite explicitly that maternity as well as paternity is sociologically determined (Malinowski, 1913, p. 179). But to the later Malinowski, who ridiculed Briffault for his notion of group motherhood (Malinowski, 1930, pp. 134-7), it would certainly have seemed absurd to talk about 'children who are not related to their mothers'. In all his Trobriand writings Malinowski was confused by a bias derived from Freudian psychology which made it impossible for him fully to distinguish relationships of a biological and psychological kind from purely sociological relationships; Malinowski's successors—notably Professor Fortes—have, I believe, been hampered by precisely this same excessive involvement in the empirical facts of the case.

Of what sort of society could we say that a child is unrelated to its mother—in the sense that there is no bond of social filiation between mother and child? Clearly the converse of the Trobriand argument applies. If there is a society in which the relation between a child and its mother is utterly unlike that between a child and its father but has much in common with the relations between cross-cousins and between brothers-in-law, then this mother/child relationship is not sensibly described as one of filiation. It is rather a relationship of affinity traced through the father.

There are many forms of ideology which might form the basis for such a pattern of ideas. The essential requirement is that the 'p' and 'q' relationships should be symbolized as different not only in quality but in kind. The Tikopia are a case in point. They say that the substance of the child originates in the father's semen and derives nothing from the body of the mother. Nevertheless the limbs of the child are fashioned by the Female Deity—a being who seems to be a mystical aspect not only of the mother herself but of her whole patrilineage (Firth, 1936, p. 481).

An analogous contrast is provided by the common Asiatic belief that the bony structure of the child's body derives from the father's semen while the soft fleshy parts are made of the blood and the milk of the mother (Lévi-Strauss, 1949, ch. xxiv). The North Burma Kachins supplement this with a metaphysical argument. They say that the child acquires its soul (*minla*) only at the moment of birth when it begins to breathe so that this soul is not in any sense derivative from the mother. For that matter the *minla* is not properly speaking hereditary at all; the child acquires this soul from its immediate environment and it is therefore important that a child be born in its father's house (Gilhodes, 1922, pp. 134, 175). Consequently a localized patrilineage is known as a *dap* (hearth), i.e. the persons born and raised in one section of one house.

In the same Assam/Burma societies which emphasize in this way the substantial unity of the child with its father's body and with its father's house, we find that the language of kinship contains a special general category which might be translated as 'affinal relatives on the wife's side'. This category includes not only all the men rated as 'wife's brother' and 'father-in-law' but also all those classed as 'mother's brother' as well as all the women classed as 'mother'. (Examples of such broad affinal categories are the Jinghpaw term *mayu* and the Lakher term *patong*—see chapters 2, 3, and 5 below.)

All these are different ways of asserting both that the '*p*' and the '*q*' relationships are radically different, and that the maternal relationship approximates to affinity, but this is not enough. Something more than metaphor and metaphysics is necessary if I am to convince you that in these societies the mother/child relationship is in sociological terms one of affinity rather than of filiation.

Fortunately, from my point of view, we possess an extremely detailed ethnography of one of these groups . . . the Lakher (Parry, 1932). Unlike some of their neighbours the Lakher recognize divorce and divorce is frequent. They consider however that the child of a properly married man is exclusively his and that his divorced wife has no rights in the child whatsoever. It follows that if a woman has a son and a daughter by two different husbands the children are deemed to be unrelated to one another. Therefore they may marry without restraint. In contrast, the son and the daughter of one man by two different mothers stand in an incestuous relationship to one another (Parry, 1932, p. 293).

This surely is the case we are looking for. Just as the Trobriands are an extreme case in the sense that the father has no consanguineous ties with his wife's children but is bound only to their mother as an affine, so also the Lakher are an extreme case in the sense that the mother has no kinship ties with her husband's children but is bound only to their father as an affine.

It would of course finally clinch the argument if I could show that the rules allow a Lakher male to marry his own divorced mother, but I am afraid that neither the Lakher nor their ethnographer seem to have considered this bizarre possibility!

However there are a variety of other Lakher customs which support my thesis. For example, the death due (*ru*) (*op. cit.* pp. 418–19) is paid on behalf of a deceased *male* by his eldest son (or other male heir) to his *pupa*, that is, to a male of the deceased's mother's patrilineage. But in the case of a deceased *female* it is paid by her husband to a male of the deceased's own patrilineage. Should her husband be dead it is payable by her youngest son. If we assume that a common logic pervades these substitutions it is evident that the payment is made from males of the husband's lineage (*ngazua*) to males of the wife's lineage (*patong*) and that the payment reasserts the survival of an affinal tie temporally severed by death. But it will be noted that in these transactions a deceased woman's son can act as deputy for her husband, that is to say, the son is deemed to be related to the mother as an affine (*ngazua*).

No *ru* is payable for unmarried persons but a different death due called *chhongchhireu* is, in this case, paid by the father of the deceased to the mother's brother of the deceased; again an indication that the mother's brother is thought of as an affinal relative (*op. cit.* p. 428). Among some Lakher groups still another death due called *chachhai* is payable by the heir of a deceased male to the deceased's wife's brother. The Lakher explained this last institution by saying that 'a man by dying has abandoned his wife so his heir must pay a fine to the dead man's relations as compensation for the inconsiderate conduct in leaving his wife without a protector'. Here again then the obligation is viewed as an aspect of affinity, and not of uterine kinship; the fact that the 'heir' in question would ordinarily be the wife's son is not considered.

Although I cannot demonstrate that the Lakher would tolerate sex relations between a man and his own mother, it is the case that among the very similar Kachin (where divorce is impossible) such relations would be treated as adultery (*shut hpyit*) rather than as incest (*jaiwawng*) (Leach, 1954, p. 137; cf. Goody, 1956a). Also in the contrary case, a Trobriand man may cohabit regularly with his own daughter or stepdaughter without committing the sin of incest (*suvasova*) even though such relations are considered morally objectionable on other grounds (Malinowski, 1932a, pp. 445–9). Malinowski says that such relations could never be legitimized as marriage but it is not clear what he means by this. A Trobriand marriage is legitimate when the wife's matrilineal kinsmen pay *urigubu* harvest gifts to the husband (cf. Powell, 1956, p. 349). In the case of a man cohabiting with his own daughter this requirement is fulfilled in any case. The Trobriand moral objection is in fact precisely on these grounds. Since the husband is already receiving *urigubu* payments on account of his wife he cannot expect to have sexual access to the daughter as well (Malinowski, 1932a, p. 446).

We should note that in both the 'extreme' cases the affinal alliance between the lineage of the father and the lineage of the mother is expressed in enduring and elaborately defined economic obligations. The require-

ment that a married Trobriand son should contribute *urigubu* harvest
gifts to his father has its counterpart in the payment due from a Lakher
male to his mother's brother and his mother's brother's sons. Both sets
of payments have their basis in a contract of marriage and are in no way
connected with any recognition of common bodily substance (Parry,
1932, p. 244).

That at any rate is my reading of the evidence, though those who dis-
agree with me can doubtless turn the matter back to front. Parry himself,
under the influence of Hutton, assumed that the peculiarities of the mother's
brother/sister's son relationship, which he recorded for the Lakher,
demonstrated 'traces of a very recent matrilineal system' (*op. cit.* p. xiii).
Although this evolutionist doctrine seems to me totally mistaken, it is
only marginally different from the views currently advocated by Fortes
(1959b) and Goody (1959). The latter (pp. 82–3) argues that, in a patrilineal system in which property is transmitted between male agnates, the
'children of the residual siblings' (i.e. the children of the sisters) are, as
it were, second class members of the patrilineage—hence the sister's son
has 'a shadowy claim' upon the property of the mother's brother by virtue
of his mother's position in his mother's brother's patrilineage. There may
well be societies where this is so but it seems to me to be going right against
the evidence to suggest that the Lakher is one of them.

I maintain on the contrary that the evidence shows unambiguously that
the obligations which link a Lakher man to his *pupa* (mother's brother or
mother's brother's son) and also to the *pupa* of his mother are part of a
complex of economic obligations established by marriage. They are obligations between males of patrilineages linked by marriage alliance and they
do *not* have their roots in notions of filiation between mother and son.

The patrilineal Lakher case is not unique of its kind. Long ago Philo
reported of the Spartans that a man might marry his mother's daughter
by a different father. McLennan, in noting this fact, deemed it incredible
and brushed it aside as an obvious ethnographic error (McLennan, 1876,
p. 177). Nevertheless McLennan's comments deserve quotation for they
show that he fully appreciated the significance of such a case. His text
has: '. . . the report of Philo, that the Spartans allowed a man to marry
his sister-uterine, but not his sister-german, or by the same father . . . we
hold it to be incredible—as discordant with old law as with the habits of
the Lacedaemonians'. But to this he adds a footnote: 'The reader may
suspect that this is a relic of strict agnatic law. But for the reasons stated
in the text, we hold that view to be excluded. *The system of relationship
through males only has never, in any well authenticated case, been developed
into such a rule as this*' (my italics).

There is also the case of the Tikopia who seem to treat cohabitation
between half-siblings of the same father as incestuous, whereas the marriage
of half-siblings of the same mother is merely odd (Firth, 1936, p. 330).
The facts here are that in Tikopia divorce and widow remarriage are both

uncommon and there is a general dislike of marriage between very close kin so that the possibility of half-sibling domestic unions does not often arise. Firth reports on two cases only. Cohabitation between half-siblings of the same father was tolerated but the union was sterile and strongly disapproved. In contrast, a domestic union of half-siblings of the same mother had produced a large and flourishing family which suffered no stigma.

No doubt the majority of human societies fall somewhere between my two extremes. Usually a child is related to both its parents because of direct ties of filiation and not simply because its parents happen to be married. I agree too that, for a substantial proportion of these intermediate cases, Fortes's concept of 'complementary filiation' may have analytical utility, but the general pattern must include the limiting extremes, so I prefer my algebraic formulation.

In a way this is all very elementary. Those of you who teach social anthropology may protest that, leaving out the algebra, this is the sort of thing we talk about to first year students in their first term. And I agree; but *because* you leave out the algebra, you have to talk about descent and filiation and extra-clan kinship and sociological paternity and so on and your pupils get more and more bewildered at every step. In contrast what I am saying is so easy that even professors ought to be able to understand! It is not algebra that is confusing but the lack of it. After all, you professionals have long been familiar with both the Trobriand and the Kachin ethnographic facts, but I suspect that you have *not* until this moment perceived that they represent two examples of the same pattern —you have been unable to perceive this because you were trapped by the conventional categories of structural classification. Now that I have pointed out the mathematical pattern the similarity is obvious. (Fig. 3, (a), (b).) But let me repeat. I am not telling you to become mathematicians. All I am asking is: Don't start off your argument with a lot of value loaded concepts which prejudge the whole issue.

The merit of putting a statement into an algebraic form is that one letter of the alphabet is as good or as bad as any other. Put the same statement into concept language, with words like paternity and filiation stuck in the middle of it, and God help you!

My time is running short and I don't suppose that I have convinced you as yet that my technique of 'generalization' really tells us anything new, but let me try again.

So far we have dealt with only half the story. My first variable 'z', which is the ratio between matrifiliation and patrifiliation, corresponds, at an ethnographic level, to variations in the ideology of genetic inheritance.

At the two extremes the Trobriand child derives its substance exclusively from its mother's blood, while the Kachin child is the bony product of its father's semen. In more normal cases where children are filiated to both parents (as with the patrilineal Tallensi) the child gets its physical substance from both parents.

But this does not take into account Malinowski's curious statement that the Trobriand child should resemble its mother's husband and nut its mother or any clan relative of the mother. Nor have I explained what Kachins are getting at when they say that the flesh and blood of a child come from its mother, though not its bone.

I won't bother you with the algebra this time but I hope you can see that if we take the Trobriand evidence to be extreme in one direction then the opposite extreme would be a society in which children resembled their mothers but not their fathers. And this is precisely what we do find. The North Burma Kachins have a patrilineal organization very similar to that of the Lakher whom I mentioned just now but, despite their patriliny, they consider that a child should resemble its mother and not its father —the exact antithesis, you see, of Malinowski's case.

In the field this baffled me completely. This was because I had too many empirical facts. The main fact was a prize pig. The Government, at enormous expense, had imported a prize Berkshire boar all the way from England. The villagers were instructed to castrate their own male pigs and have all their sows served by the boar. The boar was a sensation; no-one would talk about anything else—a regular nine days' wonder; but active co-operation in the scheme was virtually nil. It was then that I learnt that Kachin pigs derive all their physical characteristics from the sow; that being so, what on earth is the use of a prize boar?

Matrilineal pigs seemed to me a curious phenomenon so naturally I pursued the matter. I then learnt that the same thing applies to humans too—the mother feeds the child in her womb and at her breast and on that account a man's face (*myi-man*) comes from his maternal affines (this word for face, as in the Chinese equivalent, means 'reputation' as well as 'physiognomy'). The idea that appearances and reputations both come from the mother's side fits in with the idea that wives who are witches can infect by contagion both their husbands and children. The supreme manifestation of this is when a woman dies in childbirth; such a woman is deemed to be a witch of the most noxious kind and in former days all the possessions of her husband's household, including the house itself, had to be burnt so as to disinfect the community.

The crucial point to note here is that witch influence was thought to be transmitted in the food which the woman prepared—the husband was quite as liable to infection as the children. The original sources make it plain that Kachin witchcraft is contagious rather than hereditary. In structural terms Kachin witchcraft is associated with affinity, *not* filiation (Gilhodes, 1922, pp. 182-5, 296; Hanson, 1913, pp. 143f., 173-4; Leach, 1954, pp. 179f.).

If we compare this Kachin case with the Trobriand one it becomes clear that we are concerned with a single pattern of ideas which, in its general form, embodies something *other than* the notion of filiation. In both societies there is a concept of filiation which is thought of as genetic influence and is symbolized by the dogma of common substance; but there is also something different, the idea of mystical influence which can be independent of *any* tie of blood or bone.

There is more to all this than a mere quibble over the use of words and the interpretations of symbols. Fortes (1959b) has said that 'complementary filiation can be thought of as the kinship reciprocal of affinal relationship in the marriage tie', but this terminology is bound to lead to confusion. In the first place, since the phrase 'complementary filiation' only has meaning in association with unilineal descent, Fortes's argument would imply that affinal relations only occur in the presence of unilineal descent, which is plainly absurd. But secondly, in view of the distinction which Fortes draws between filiation and descent his formula amounts to an assertion that 'affinal relationship in the marriage tie' is a category applicable only to relations between individuals. But empirically this is not the case. The Jinghpaw expression *mayu/dama* and analagous categories elsewhere denote relationships of enduring affinal alliance between whole groups of persons. It is quite misleading to think of such group relationship as 'reciprocal' of any particular relationship between an individual parent and an individual child.

In Chapter 3 of this book I show how such relations of enduring affinal alliance are expressed in the transfer of goods and in notions of differential political status. But here I am referring to something both more general and more metaphysical. My proposition is that the relationship which we denote by the word 'affinity' is very commonly given cultural expression as 'mystical influence', but that this in turn is only a special instance of something more general, the logical opposition between unity through incorporation and unity through alliance.

In each of my examples (Fig. 3) we see that certain ideas cluster together to form a pattern (a topological 'set'), and the elements in the pattern divide up to form a category opposition. Thus with Trobrianders—mystical influence is linked with physical appearance but opposed to blood relationship. With Kachins—mystical influence is linked with physical appearance, flesh and food but opposed to bone relationship. With Tallensi—genetic influence is associated with blood *and* bone *and* physical appearance and can be derived from both parents, but this is opposed to a form of mystical influence called *tyuk* and a tendency to witchcraft, both of which are derived from the mother's relatives only. In this last case the opposed categories overlap but even so, as Fortes shows clearly, the two kinds of influence, the genetic and the mystical, are, in the Tallensi view, quite distinct (Fortes, 1949, p. 35; also index refs. to *yin*).

The category distinctions involved in these different cases are all of much the same kind but they are *not* identical and it would be misleading to try to fit them into a typology by tagging them with precisely defined labels such as filiation, descent and affinity. Instead I suggest that the facts can be generalized into a formula which would run something like this:

'A marriage creates an alliance between two groups, A and B. The children of the marriage may be related to either or both of these groups by incorporation, either permanent or partial, but they can also be related to either or both the groups by virtue of the marriage alliance itself. The symbols I have been discussing—of bone and blood and flesh and food and mystical influence, discriminate on the one hand between permanent and partial incorporation, and on the other between incorporation and alliance. These are variables which are significant in all societies and not merely in unilineal systems of a particular type.'

The value of such generalization is that it invites us to re-examine familiar material from a fresh point of view. For example, my cases indicate that the distinction between incorporation and alliance is always expressed in the difference between common substance and mystical influence—and surely, this is just what the Tikopia are talking about when a man refers to his own son as *tama* (child) but to the son of his

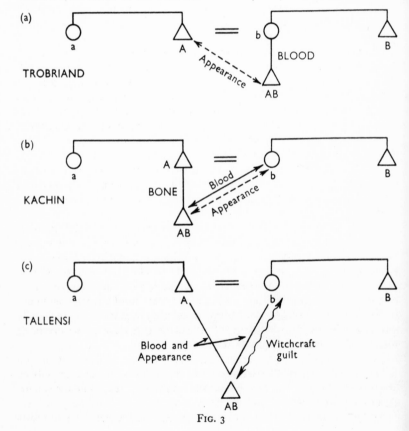

FIG. 3

sister's husband as *tama tapu* (sacred child)? But you won't find that recorded in the pages of *We, the Tikopia*.

Perhaps I may elaborate that point. The exceptional detail of Firth's ethnographic material is a standing invitation for every reader to try to 'rethink' the particular explanations which Firth himself offers us. Firth's discussion of the *tuatina/tama tapu* (mother's brother/sister's son) relationship is very extensive but nowhere does it serve to explain why the latter should carry the epithet 'sacred child'. Firth's general position seems to be similar to that adopted by Goody in the article which I have criticized above; the reader of *We, the Tikopia* gets the impression that the sister's son has a sort of second class membership in Ego's patrilineage (ramage) and that the relationship is one which Fortes and Goody would describe as 'extra-clan kinship'. As I understand it, Firth considers that the gifts which the *tama tapu* receives from his *tuatina* originate in rights of inheritance based in some kind of principle of descent (Firth, 1936, pp. 224–5, 279ff.). Yet this hardly seems consistent with the fact that although a man has certain rights of usufruct in land belonging to his mother's patrilineage, he loses these rights as soon as his mother is dead (*op. cit.* p. 391).

In contrast I would suggest that the description 'sacred child' has a logical fit with the notion that the child is formed in the mother's womb by the Female Deity associated with the mother's patrilineage (*op. cit.* p. 481) and that the same Female Deity has temporary charge over a man's soul during the intricate processes of transition from life to death (Firth, 1955, p. 17). This implies surely that the sister's child has a mystical rather than a substantial link with members of Ego's patrilineage? Firth's meticulously detailed record of Tikopian attitudes towards the *tuatina/ tama tapu* relationship seems fully in accord with this. The Tikopia themselves appear to regard this relationship as an affinal link between whole lineages rather than as a simple tie between individuals (Firth, 1936, p. 213).

But let me repeat. Polemic apart, the principal generalized hypothesis which has so far emerged from this essay is that, in *any* system of kinship and marriage, there is a fundamental ideological opposition between the relations which endow the individual with membership of a 'we group' of some kind (relations of incorporation), and those other relations which link 'our group' to other groups of like kind (relations of alliance), and that, in this dichotomy, relations of incorporation are distinguished symbolically as relations of common substance, while relations of alliance are viewed as metaphysical influence.

The first part of this hypothesis has obvious links with the distinction between the 'internal' system and the 'external' system which has been stressed by Homans (1951) and by Fortes (1959b, p. 194). The latter part, though related to Fortes (1959a,) is novel.

At first sight it might be supposed that the proposition is readily dis-

proved, for although it is true that in many societies the threat of supernatural attack ('metaphysical influence') is expected to come from 'out-
siders'—notably affinal kin and political associates—there are well known
instances where the contrary is the case. Thus, in matrilineal Ashanti, the
witch is habitually a lineage kinsman (Rattray, 1927, p. 30) and the same
is true of the patrilineal Tiv (Bohannan, 1953, p. 85). Furthermore
throughout patrilineal Polynesia it is the father's sister who must be
particularly respected lest she invoke supernatural sanctions (Firth, 1936,
p. 222; Mabuchi, 1958).

But my proposition is not quite so easily disposed of. The 'mystical
influence' which has been discussed in this paper is of the same kind as
that which we English denote by the word Fate, which the Tallensi
denote by the term *yin,* and which Fortes has distinguished under the
phrase 'prenatal destiny' (Fortes, 1959a). It is a power beyond human
control. My thesis—and here for once Professor Fortes and I seem to be
in agreement—is that in any particular case the ideas concerning such
uncontrolled mystical influence must serve to specify something about the
social structure. An individual is thought to be subject to certain kinds of
mystical influence because of the structural position in which he finds
himself and not because of the intentional malice or favour of any other
individual.

Doctrines of this sort are quite distinct from those which credit particular individuals with the capacity to punish wrongdoers or attack their
enemies by secret supernatural means.

Some examples will serve to illustrate this distinction.

In the ideology of Kachin witchcraft the witch is presumed to be an
unconscious and involuntary agent; she brings disaster upon her husband
and her children, not because she wishes to to do so, but because she has the
misfortune to be the host of a witch spirit (*hpyi*). She is a person tainted
with contagion through no fault of her own and hence (in my terminology)
she affects her victims through 'uncontrolled mystical influence'. Contrast
with this the Ashanti doctrine which presumes that witches are adult
persons, fully conscious of their misdeeds, who receive special training
and initiation into their nefarious arts (Rattray, 1927, pp. 28–31).

This Ashanti witchcraft is not 'uncontrolled mystical influence' in my
sense of the term but a form of 'controlled supernatural attack'. In this
respect it is analagous to such conceptions as the threat of the father's
sister's curse in Samoa, or the threat of the chief's sorcery in the Trobriands and Tikopia; the individuals who wield such *controlled* supernatural authority are persons who command respect (Mead, 1930, p. 146;
1934, pp. 309, 310, 314, 356; Firth, 1936, p. 222; Malinowski, 1932b,
p. 85f.; Firth, 1959, p. 145).

Monica Wilson's Nyakyusa material brings out this distinction very
clearly. In Nyakyusa belief 'good' and 'bad' witchcraft are both regarded
as forms of 'controlled supernatural attack', but whereas a bad witch

acquires his witchcraft unconsciously by influence from his father's wife, a good witch ('defender') *acquires* his witchcraft intentionally by taking medicines (Wilson, 1949, pp. 24, 98–102).

Kachin evidence illustrates the same point in a different way. Kachins carry out 'controlled supernatural attack' by invoking the Spirit of Cursing, called *Mātsa Kānu* (Gilhodes, 1922, pp. 292–3). This name is a combination of two kinship categories *tsa* (father-in-law, mother's brother) and *nu* (mother); it embodies a formulation of the Kachin theory that the power of cursing and the power of witchcraft are of the same kind and emanate from the same source—namely the affinal relatives on the mother's side (*mayu*). The witch emits this power *unconsciously* having been infected by an uncontrolled mystical influence: the man who curses an opponent invokes precisely the same power but does so *consciously*.

As a demonstration that my procedure of topological generalization has some practical utility I propose now to develop this distinction so as to provide a gloss on one of the classical topics of anthropological theory.

Anthropologists have a wide and varied range of functionalist explanations as to why custom should so often require a man to display some special, rather bizarre, form of behaviour towards a father's sister or a mother's brother. Mostly these explanations focus in arguments about ambiguities in principles of descent and rights of inheritance (e.g. Goody, 1959). Each type of explanation throws illumination on appropriately selected case material but none of them are at all convincing as contributions to general theory. The material which I have now presented suggests that the whole topic might fruitfully be considered from quite a new point of view, namely the degree of coincidence between notions of 'uncontrolled mystical influence' on the one hand and notions of 'controlled supernatural attack' on the other. These opposed variables may be thought of as forming a topological set.

For brevity let us denote 'uncontrolled mystical influence' by the symbol x and 'controlled supernatural attack' by the symbol y and then consider the incidence of the x and y notions as reported from the societies which we have been discussing throughout this paper.

TIKOPIA:	x and y are separated. x comes from the mother; y from the father's sister.
LAKHER (KACHIN):	x and y coincide, both come from the *patong* (*mayu*), that is the mother's brother's patrilineage.
TROBRIANDS:	x and y do not necessarily coincide but may do so. x comes from the father; y comes from affinal relatives (as an expression of malice) or from the chief (as an expression of legitimate authority).
ASHANTI:	x and y are separated. x comes from the father; y from adult women of Ego's matrilineage.
TALLENSI:	x and y are separated. x derives from uterine kin; y from Ego's patrilineal ancestors.

C

This pattern variation is far from random, for the degree of coincidence between x and y corresponds to the degree to which affinal alliance plays a part in the ongoing political structure of the society. As is shown in Chapters 3 and 5 of this book the Kachin and the Lakher are societies in which the affinal ties of chiefs and lineage headmen have a structural permanence comparable to that provided by the idea of lineage perpetuity in unilineal descent systems. In contrast among the Tikopia, the Tallensi and the Ashanti there are no 'relations of perpetual affinity' which can serve to express enduring political relations of superordination and subordination. But in this respect the Trobrianders provide an intermediate case, for, while they have no ideal of permanent affinal relationship, they use the *urigubu* harvest payment, which is normally an obligation due to affines, as a device for expressing the tributary obligations of a village headman to his chief.

The general inference therefore is that, where x and y coincide, relations of affinity are being used to express political dominance.

The reader who wishes to verify my algebraic generalizations for himself will find the following references useful:

TIKOPIA

Evidence concerning the father's sister's curse and the mystical influence of the Female Deity has been cited above. In Tikopia the form of marriage serves to emphasize its lack of *political* importance. Once a marriage has been established a rather complex set of obligations is set up between the lineage of the husband and the lineage of the wife, but the marriage itself purports to be a 'marriage by capture' in which the parents of the bride remain ignorant of what is afoot until all is *fait accompli*. This marriage by capture is 'characteristic mainly of chiefly families' (Firth, 1936, p. 539), and seems to amount to an explicit denial that the chiefs are using marriage for political ends.

LAKHER

Parry (1932, pp. 244–5): 'It is *ana* (taboo) for a maternal uncle to curse or insult his nephew. . . . The highest term of respect in use among the Lakhers is *papu* (my maternal uncle) not *ipa* (my father); a villager addressing the chief always calls him *papu*.' Kachin behaviour is similar; a chief is addressed as *tsa* (mother's brother). *Tsa* possess particular potency at cursing (*mǎtsa*); for references regarding the political significance of Lakher marriage alliances see Chapter 5 below.

TROBRIANDS

Malinowski (1932a, p. 137): 'It is characteristic of their ideas of the bonds of marriage and fatherhood which they regard as artificial and untrustworthy under any strain that the principle suspicion of sorcery attaches always to the wife and children.'

Here the mystical influence of father over children is separated from the controlled supernatural attack of children against father. On the other hand *ibid.* p. 190 shows the father to be in control of female sorcerers who are liable (unless the father is properly placated) to attack his pregnant daughter, and in numerous contexts we are told how the chief exercises his authority with the aid of professional sorcerers who obey his command (e.g. Malinowski, 1932b, pp. 85–6). Here the mystical influence of the father may coincide with the supernatural attack of the father-chief.

It should be remarked that the chief's relationship to his village headmen is typically that of father (*tama*) or brother-in-law (*lubou*). The tribute which a chief receives from his political subordinates is, from another point of view, the *urigubu* (harvest payment) paid to a father or to a brother-in-law (Malinowski, 1935, I, pp. 392–7, 414; Powell, 1956, pp. 481).

ASHANTI

For ideas about supernatural attack see Rattray (1923, chapter 2; 1927, pp. 28–31). Ashanti often marry near kin and approve of reciprocal cross-cousin marriage. In traditional Ashanti this was carried to the extreme that the royal family and also certain professional guilds had an almost caste-like aspect (Rattray, 1923, p. 301; 1927, chapters xxix, xxx). However this type of small group endogamy did not result in a structure in which ties of marriage alliance could serve political ends.

TALLENSI

For ideas about supernatural influence see especially Fortes (1959a) and the references to *yin* in Fortes (1949). Since a Tallensi may not marry any near kins-woman, however she be related, it is self evident that marriage cannot here serve as a relationship of perpetual political alliance in the sense which I have been discussing.

This finding has a bearing upon the argument of Fortes (1959a), for, with certain qualifications, Fortes's Oedipus theology corresponds to my x ('uncontrolled mystical influence'), while his Job theology corresponds to my y ('controlled supernatural attack'). In the West African examples which Fortes has discussed, x and y are complementary notions which tend to cancel out—the inescapable consequences of personal Fate modify the arbitrary dictates of an all powerful God and *vice versa*, but my additional evidence shows that this seeming balance is fortuitous. There are some societies where Fate and Implacable Deity are to be found personified in one and the same affinal personality, and in such cases the relation between religious ideas and political authority takes on a very different and very special aspect—the *mana* of the King and the *mana* of the witch coalesce in the person of the all powerful Father-in-Law.

Without the algebra, my x/y proposition reads thus: '*uncontrolled mystical influence* denotes a relation of alliance; *controlled supernatural attack* denotes a relation of potential authority of attacker over attacked or *vice versa*. Where the presumed source of *controlled supernatural attack* is the same as the presumed source of *uncontrolled mystical influence* that source is in a position of political authority vis-à-vis Ego.' In this form we have an hypothesis which might, in principle, be subjected to test. In practice I suspect that the establishment of convincing negative instances may prove rather elusive. For example the material which Firth has recently provided about the relation between spirit mediums and their familiars in Tikopia and elsewhere looks at first sight as if it ought to provide an excellent test case, but I rather think that, so far as my hypo-thesis is concerned, this particular evidence could be interpreted in several different ways (Firth, 1959, pp. 141–6). But here at any rate is a matter which invites investigation.

This whole digression into the structural implications of metaphysical belief has been introduced only by way of illustration. The insights which emerge relate to facts which cut right across the conventional categories of anthropological discussion and my objective has been to demonstrate by example how an excessive interest in the classification of ethnographic facts serves to obscure rather than to illuminate our perception of social reality. And here I revert to the point from which I started.

I am constantly amazed by the feats of mental gymnastic which anthropologists perform in their efforts of produce universal definitions and discriminations; notable examples are Gough's definition of marriage (Gough, 1959, p. 32) and Fortes's discrimination between filiation, affinity and descent (Fortes, 1959b). My harsh view is that the value of such butterfly collecting activity is quite ephemeral and that the categories which result from it should always be highly suspect. This applies equally to the vague topological entities of my own analysis and to the polished concepts of Professor Fortes. We need to understand that the establishment of classifying categories is never more than a temporary *ad hoc* expedient. Most such categories have ceased to serve any useful purpose long before they achieve the distinction of appearing in print.

So far as our immediate discussion is concerned I readily admit that, in any given social system, we shall always find some kind of notion of corporate kinship which stands opposed to some kind of notion of marriage alliance as p is to q, but what we can usefully compare as between different societies are not these particular ps and qs (regarded as separate institutions) but the ratio of p to q considered as a mathematical function. Or, in non-metrical language, we need to think of the relationships which link children to their parents and the parents to one another as constituting a 'neighbourhood system'—a topological space.

No doubt many of you will want to dismiss my whole argument as a futile exercise in bogus mathematics. I don't accept that. I believe that we social anthropologists are like the mediaeval Ptolemaic astronomers; we spend our time trying to fit the facts of the objective world into the framework of a set of concepts which have been developed *a priori* instead of from observation.

It is some years since Professor Firth drew attention to the alarming proliferation of structuralist terminology. He noted with dismay that maximal, major and minimal lineages had been supplemented by medial, inner and nuclear lineages; effective lineages were distinguished from morphological lineages; social relations had acquired focal fields, vertebral principles and constellations of ties and cleavages (Firth, 1951a).

That was in 1951, but the process has continued. We now have not merely filiation but complementary filiation, not merely siblings but residual siblings. Of such cycles and epicycles there is no end.

The trouble with Ptolemaic astronomy was not that it was wrong but that it was sterile—there could be no real development until Galileo was prepared to abandon the basic premise that celestial bodies must of necessity move in perfect circles with the earth at the centre of the universe.

We anthropologists likewise must re-examine basic premises and realize that English language patterns of thought are not a necessary model for the whole of human society.

Malinowski's basic premiss was that the elementary family is a universal institution. Fortes would qualify this but retains a dogmatic view of the functional utility of incest which is very similar to Malinowski's. This leads logically to an acceptance of English categories and to the assumption that our words consanguinity and affinity have some universal value. It is this which leads anthropologists to treat the words sibling, filiation, descent and affinity as absolute technical terms which can be distinguished from one another by *a priori* reasoning without reference to ethnographic evidence.

My contrary thesis is that ethnographic facts will be much easier to understand if we approach them free of *all* such *a priori* assumptions. Our concern is with what the significant social categories are; not with what they ought to be.

If you feel you must start with assumptions then let them be logical (that is mathematical) assumptions—such as that the social relation between brothers must of necessity be in some sense the opposite of the social relation between brothers-in-law. But do not drag in private psychological theories behind a smoke screen of technical terms.

All I have tried to do here is to show that an unprejudiced re-examination of established ethnographic facts which does *not* start off with a battery of concepts thought up in a professorial study may lead to some unexpected conclusions.

And that must be my conclusion—stick to the facts of the case, and exercise your imagination; but don't get so personally involved in the situation that you cannot distinguish between the empirical facts and your private analytic concepts.

In this first Malinowski Memorial lecture I have set out to demonstrate, from a single small example, that Malinowski still has no rival in the penetration of his ethnographic observation. Where Malinowski's work was limited was that it was too exclusively Trobriand; his theoretical concepts were designed to fit Trobriand data just as, latterly, Fortes's concepts have been designed to fit Tallensi and Ashanti data. But it is still possible to base speculative generalizations on Malinowski's facts, and I believe that speculative generalization, even if it often proves wrong, is very well worth while. Even from tonight's popshy we may have learnt a little.

2

Jinghpaw Kinship Terminology

an experiment in Ethnographic Algebra

INTRODUCTORY NOTE

THIS paper first appeared in the *J.R.A.I.* Vol. 75 (1945). Certain parts of the argument are explicitly contrary to those put forward in Chapter 1 of this book and I reprint the article here with the express purpose of emphasizing my shift of viewpoint.

In 1945 I was still dominated by the views of Malinowski and I accepted uncritically the biographical approach to kinship advocated by Malinowski in *The Sexual Life of Savages.* This led me directly into self contradiction. I started off sensibly enough (p. 32, Rule 1) by saying that in the investigation of kinship terminologies the principle of Occam's Razor must certainly apply, but I then sought to accommodate myself to Malinowski's dogma that the elementary family is a universal institution of universally paramount importance. This Malinowskian doctrine is propounded in Rule 2, but since it contradicts Rule 1 it had to be contradicted again in Rule 5! As should be obvious from other chapters of this book, I do not any longer look upon the elementary family as a universal institution of fixed type. Were I to write this article now in the same bizarre form as before, I should drop our Rule 2 altogether and reduce Rule 5 to:

'The child will be taught to discriminate the members of its own patrilocal group on the basis of sex and age.'

The criticism of Professor Fortes's concept of 'complementary filiation' which I have developed above in Chapter 1 reflects this shift of viewpoint. In particular the argument under Rule 2 (pp. 32–3) implies that in *all* societies the two relationships father/child and mother/child have important elements in common such as are indicated by the English language expression parent/child. This view I would now explicitly repudiate (*supra* p. 10: cf. Leach, 1960).

In another respect also I now consider that my presentation of the facts in this essay is open to very serious objection. The principles of classification which I have assumed to be relevant are those of sex, age and place of residence, but I would now argue, as in Chapter 1, that in certain cases the essential key to understanding is to perceive that a particular relationship '*p*' is *the opposite of* another relationship '*q*'. Thus for this Jinghpaw system a great deal of circumlocution might have been avoided if I had displayed the following relationships as pairs of opposites:

Relational category 'p'	Associated Behaviour	Relational category 'q'	Associated Behaviour
1. hkau/hkau	co-operative equality	hpu/nau (male)	restraint, inequality.
2. ning/ning	co-operative equality	na/nau (female)	restraint, inequality.
3. rat/rat	restraint, equality	hpu/nau (female)	restraint, inequality.
4. nu/sha	affection, intimacy	moi/nam na/nau (male)	respect, near avoidance.
5. tsa/hkri (female)	'illicit relationship' flirtation	gu/nam (female)	'lawful relationship' embarrassment, avoidance.
6. tsa/hkri (male)	prototype of mayu/dama affinal authority	wa/sha	prototype of lineage authority.

In particular, the evasive explanation of the category *moi* (p. 38) and the equally evasive footnote 1 on page 39 would then have been unnecessary.

The behaviour qualities attaching to most of these relationships are discussed in greater detail in Leach (1954, 136–40) but on one of these further comment may be made. It is an ancient tradition that lovers should address one another in poetry by the 'illicit relationship' terms *tsa* and *hkri* (i.e. 'mother's brother'/'sister's daughter'); in post-war journalism this usage has become debased and in an amorous context the words have now come to mean 'boy friend' and 'girl friend' respectively! When both parties are males the relationship is still one of extreme respect from *hkri* to *tsa*.

In current British anthropology the study of kinship terminologies is decidedly out of fashion and I certainly do not regard myself as a staunch upholder of the Morgan–Rivers–Radcliffe-Brown tradition with which such studies are commonly associated. But if the study of kinship terminology is often overvalued it is not valueless. I would claim that both this paper and my later study of Trobriand kinship terminology (Leach, 1958) display sociological facts of some importance which it would be very difficult to demonstrate by any other means.

* * * * *

SECTION I: THEORY

Kinship systems have a perennial fascination. From Morgan's day to the present, a long succession of authors have produced their diagrams and algebraic explanations. Indeed the explanations are so many and varied that it is possible to suspect that this particular type of jig-saw puzzle fits together in several different ways.

In an important paper Professor Radcliffe-Brown (1941) has recently discussed two such ways, which he labels respectively 'conjectural history' and 'structural analysis' (p. 1). Whether the argument which follows can rightly be held to fall into either category I find it hard to determine.

Granted that the objective of the social anthropologist is the elucidation of general laws concerning the nature of human society, the particular study of kinship systems may prove deceptively attractive. Kinship terminology and its diagrammatic arrangement provide, ready-made, a delightful series of mathematical abstractions and it is all too easy to develop their analysis into a 'system' having little relation to sociological facts. In another recent paper Radcliffe-Brown (1940) has remarked that 'if in an Australian tribe I observe in a number of instances the behaviour towards one another of persons who stand in the relation of mother's brother and sister's son, it is in order that I may be able to record as precisely as possible the general or normal form of this relationship, abstracted from the variations of particular instances, though taking into account those variations' (p. 4).

I would suggest, however, that the existence of any 'general or normal form' cannot be taken for granted, but must be demonstrated. In this quotation, the 'persons who stand in the relation of mother's brother and sister's son' might be taken to mean either persons standing in that blood relationship, biologically defined, or persons categorized by a particular pair of native kinship terms. Identification of these two meanings may lead to confusion. To me it seems that many of the artificial dogmas that have arisen during the development of kinship theory have their source in too great a readiness to translate native terminology into what is arbitrarily deemed to be the primary English equivalent. The focal point of apparent norms may thereby be displaced. For example, in the system I shall describe, the mother's brother and the wife's father fall into the same term category, *tsa*, which includes also other relatives. There may be a norm of behaviour which characterizes a man's attitude towards his *tsa*, but it is not legitimate to assume that this characteristic attitude is especially typical either of the respect for a mother's brother or of that for a wife's father.

In my own field work, I have found the determination of sociological norms extremely difficult, and at no level of analysis would such a norm coincide with the cultural ideal put forward by a good informant, well versed in native law and custom. The field worker has three distinct 'levels' of behaviour pattern to consider. The first is the actual behaviour of individuals. The average of all such individual behaviour patterns constitutes the second, which may fairly be described as 'the norm'. But there is a third pattern, the native's own description of himself and his society, which constitutes 'the ideal'.[1] Because the field worker's time is short and he must rely upon a limited number of informants, he is always tempted to identify the second of these patterns with the third. Clearly the norm is strongly influenced by the ideal, but I question whether the two are ever precisely coincident. In the study of kinship this

---

[1] cf. Malinowski (1932a, p. 120); also Gordon Brown and Barnett (1942, p. 30). The latter speak of 'ideal', 'anticipated' and 'actual' behaviour.

is an important distinction, because any structural analysis of a kinship system is necessarily a discussion of ideal behaviour, not of normal behaviour.

In the account which follows, the 'explanation' of Jinghpaw kinship terminology rests on a rule of preferred marriage. The reader should remember throughout that the preference is for marriage between *gu* and *nam* (and not, let us say, for marriage between a 'father's sister's son', and a 'mother's brother's daughter'). This marriage rule is an item of ideal behaviour with mythological sanction, but it cannot be regarded as a statistical norm of behaviour, nor even as an element of conjectural history. I see no reason to suppose that in the past the norm was any closer to the ideal than I have found it to be to-day. In short, while I claim to demonstrate that the rule in question has a functional significance in the society as it now exists, I am not concerned with any teleological argument as to whether the marriage rule is causal to the form of society, or vice versa.

I seek to show that Jinghpaw kinship terminology, which is superficially extremely complex, would appear simple and consistent to a man living in an ideal society, organized according to certain very simple rules. These rules constitute the ideal pattern of Jinghpaw society, to which the actual society is now, and probably always has been, a somewhat remote approximation.

I will first demonstrate that in a hypothetical society organized in accordance with seven structural principles, the terminology actually used by the Jinghpaw Kachins is the simplest possible. Consider a hypothetical society organized as follows:

Hypothesis 1.—Descent is patrilineal.

Hypothesis 2.—Marriage is patrilocal (that is, a man always continues to live in the house of his father, while a woman, on marriage, leaves her own home and goes to that of her husband).

Hypothesis 3.—Each patrilineal-patrilocal group is exogamous.

Hypothesis 4.—Polygyny is permissible; polyandry is not.

Hypothesis 5.—All women marry immediately upon reaching puberty; therefore the patrilineal-patrilocal group at no time contains *adult* females who have been born into that group.

Hypothesis 6.—A man must always marry a woman from the original patrilineal-patrilocal group of his own mother; and that woman must not be older than himself.

Hypothesis 7.—A woman can never be given in marriage to a man from the original patrilineal-patrilocal group of her own mother; she will always be given in marriage to a man of the patrilocal group into which her father's sister has already married.

Hypothesis 5 is an exaggeration introduced for purposes of simplified demonstration. Hypotheses 6 and 7 are logically identical; they are given separately here because, while a modified permissive form of Hyp. 6 is

common to many actual societies, it is the negative (incest) aspect of
Hyp. 7 which is most heavily stressed in the Jinghpaw reality. If 'may'
were substituted for 'must' in Hyp. 6, we could find a wide range of
societies which approximate to the pattern of Hyp. 1–6, but the ban on
marriage to the father's sister's daughter, stressed in Hyp. 7, is relatively
rare. The principle involved has been described by some writers as
'asymmetrical descent', and is found, here and there, in all parts of the
world.[1] But clearly no actual society could conform rigidly to the ideal
pattern here laid down.

Granted these hypothetical conditions, our problem is to devise a
system of kinship terminology which, *in the simplest manner possible*, will
be logically consistent with the given conditions. It is necessary first to
specify the rules of classification which I intend to apply and then to try
to justify the claim that these rules are the simplest possible in the circumstances.[2]

Rule 1.—Two distinct terms will never be used where one can serve. A
speaker will only differentiate terminologically between two individuals if
failure to do so would imply a situation either contrary to the listed hypotheses or contrary to the universal law of incest (the ban on sexual relations
between parent and child, and between brother and sister).

The primacy and universality of the biological human family has
repeatedly been stressed by both anthropologists and psychologists. It is
in any case generally conceded that relationships within the biological
family are, of all relationships, by far the most significant psychologically,
the most highly charged with emotion.[3] From this fact we derive

Rule 2.—In any patrilineal kinship system, the only sentiments which
may be claimed as universal are those associated with the elementary human
family, namely: father-child, mother-child, brother-brother, brother-sister,

[1] Of the extensive literature on asymmetrical cross-cousin marriage I may
mention Frazer (1918), vol. ii, pp. 98ff.; Westermarck (1921), vol. ii, pp. 68–79;
Hodson (1925); Seligman (1928); Bose (1937); Shaw (1928), p. 140; Roy (1936),
p. 141; Parry (1932), p. 293; Cameron (1911), p. xviii. (See also Chapter 3 *infra*.)
Mrs Seligman has suggested that the phenomenon of asymmetry represents a
subordinated matriliny in a patrilineal society. Bose, Parry and others hold similar
views. This is clearly conjectural history. No doubt societies exist in which both
patrilineal and matrilineal lineage have a social function, but, so far as I can judge,
Jinghpaw society is not one of them.
[2] Such rules are of great importance; in relation to field work data, they represent
the inferred 'structural principles' upon which Radcliffe-Brown lays such stress,
although I am not suggesting that Radcliffe-Brown would approve of the form in
which they are here presented. Cf. also Tax (1937), pp. 18–32.
[3] Thus, Radcliffe-Brown (1941): 'The existence of the elementary family
creates three special kinds of social relationship, that between parent and child,
that between children of the same parents (siblings), and that between husband
and wife as parents of the same child or children' (p. 2). Malinowski (1932) has
urged that in a matrilineal society the relationship between mother's brother and
sister's child is equally fundamental (pp. 5–6). [But see above p. 28.]

sister-sister. Where terms exist to identify such relationships, they may legitimately be presumed to represent sentiments at least broadly analogous to those covered by the English terms.[1]

Sociologically speaking, the sex of a small child is usually irrelevant to its elders, and there is nothing in our hypotheses to suggest the contrary. From this fact derives Rule 3:

Rule 3.—An elder addressing a child will make no distinction as to sex, unless the implications of the listed hypotheses demand it.

A corollary of Rules 1 and 3 is Rule 4:

Rule 4.—Except where it is contrary to hypothesis, an adult woman will address any child by the same term as does her husband.

In Rule 1, I have assumed that a child distinguishes between the members of its own biological family on a basis of (*a*) sex, and (*b*) age status. To the adult, the essential difference between the father and the elder brother rests on the biological connection, but this the child cannot comprehend. To the child, the difference is rather one of behaviour, of appearance, of authority. The classifications natural to a child in considering its elders derive from a sentimental enlargement of this axiomatic principle.[2] The limits of extension of the basic sentiment are defined by our hypotheses, especially Hyp. 2, 3, 6, and 7. Hence:

Rule 5.—For the child, terms applicable to members of the speaker's own biological family (see Rule 2) will be extended to other persons living within the same patrilocal group, the extension being made on the basis of sex and age: such terms will not be extended to persons living outside the speaker's own patrilocal group.

Rule 6.—A term applied to a member of any patrilocal group other than the speaker's own will apply also to all other persons of the same group, of similar sex and age status.

It must be emphasized that these last two rules are meant here to apply only to the special conditions of our hypothetical society. In practice they apply to a wide range of societies organized on an exogamous, patrilineal lineage basis.[3]

Two other special differentiations derive from Hyp. 7:

[1] In no other case can it be assumed that any term has a primary meaning which can be exactly translated into an English equivalent. The significance of all other relationships is dependent upon structural factors in the particular society under consideration. There are even some societies employing a markedly descriptive terminology, where specific terms for brother and sister are lacking, e.g., the Yoruba (see von Werder, 1939, pp. 223-4). Again, in practice, legal fictions may override the basic biological unity, as in the distinction between *pater* and *genitor* among the Nuer (see Evans-Pritchard, 1945).

[2] cf. Radcliffe-Brown's 'unity of the sibling group' (1941, p. 7).

[3] These rules imply the structural principle of 'bifurcate merging' described by Lowie (1929), which is said to have a high correlation with clan organization.

Rule 7.—Among members of the opposite sex in patrilocal groups other than the speaker's own, the child must distinguish between persons with whom marriage will be permitted and those with whom it will be forbidden.

Rule 8.—For a male child, the potential wife's father, and for a female child, the potential husband are males of potential authority status. The *child* must distinguish such classes of persons from all others.

With the exception of members of the speaker's own biological family, the precise blood relationship between any two individuals is, generally speaking, irrelevant. In the hypothetical society under consideration relationship is defined by:

(*a*) The patrilineal-patrilocal group into which the individual is born.

(*b*) The patrilocal group in which the individual resides.

(*c*) The permissibility of sex relations.

(*d*) In the case of males, the age-group status of the individual in the line of patrilineal descent.

Let us now consider five distinct patrilineal-patrilocal groups, designated AA, A, B, C, and CC, respectively, which conform to the required conditions. Men of AA always take their wives from A; men of A take their wives from B; men of B take their wives from C; men of C take their wives from CC. At any given instant the community resident in B will consist of:

(i) Adult males who were born into B.

(ii) The wives of B males, who by birth are adult females of C.

(iii) The children of B males and C females of either sex.

There will be no adult females of B group birth still resident in B; by Hyp. 5, all such are now married and resident in A.

Let us construct a terminology adequate for the use of a child born into B. In place of symbols we will use the monosyllables of the Jinghpaw terminology.

First, from Rule 2, we need terms with the primary biological meanings: mother (*nu*), father (*wa*), brother (*hpu*), sister (*na*). By Rule 5, these terms can be extended to other persons resident in B, as follows:

Definition 1: *wa*. The real father, and all other males of the father's age group resident within the speaker's own group, are addressed as *wa*.

Definition 2: *nu*. The real mother, and all other women of the mother's age group resident within the speaker's own group, are addressed as *nu*.

Definition 3: *hpu*. All males of the speaker's own age group belonging to the speaker's own group by birth, are addressed as *hpu*.

Definition 4: *na*. All females of the speaker's own age group belonging to the speaker's own group by birth, are addressed as *na*.

Though of the same age group, *hpu* and *na* are necessarily older than the child speaker, since we presume that the latter, when first learning to talk is the younger of any pair of persons in reciprocal speech relationship.

A theoretical point which may be stressed is that a kinship term in isolation has no significance; it is the relationship expressed by a pair of reciprocal terms which has structural importance and which can be interpreted in terms of behaviour.[1] Any particular term (T) may have a variety of different reciprocals (R, R', R'', etc.), and the relationship denoted by T-R has not necessarily much in common with the relationship T-R'. Nevertheless, in view of the rules set out above, we are here concerned with only two forms of reciprocal, namely, relationships of the form T-R, where the sex of T and R are both defined, and relationships of the form T-R', where the sex of T is defined but that of R' is not.

Reverting to our hypothesis, we require reciprocals for the four terms already defined. Applying Rules 3 and 4, we see that two reciprocals are sufficient.

Definition 5: *sha*. *Wa* and *nu* address the speaker as *sha*, irrespective of sex.

Definition 6: *nau*. *Hpu* and *na* address the speaker as *nau*, irrespective of sex.

The term *nau*, thus defined, might almost be translated as 'youngster'. The child itself will in due course use the same term to address infants of its own patrilocal group, younger than itself.[2]

Within the child's own patrilocal group there still remain the members of age groups senior to *wa* and *nu* (Def. 1, 2). Without considering factors of behaviour, it may be seen from purely algebraic arguments that in the given conditions the extension of any of the terms already defined to members of the second ascending generation would be inappropriate. Since the sex of *sha* is indeterminate (Def. 5) and the sex of the children of *sha* will be indeterminate (Rule 3), we logically require a term of relationship T-R', which covers four reciprocal biological relationships: father's father—son's son, father's father—son's daughter, mother's father—daughter's son, mother's father—daughter's daughter. Of these, however, mother's father, daughter's daughter, and daughter's son are not members of the speaker's own patrilocal group, hence (according to Rule 5) none of the terms so far defined can be extended to cover these categories. Since a child distinguishes the sex of its elders, father's father must be distinct from father's mother. Hence three new terms are required:

Definition 7: *ji*. Males whom the father addresses as *wa*, or *ji*, are addressed as *ji*.

Definition 8: *woi*. Females whom the father addresses as *nu*, or *woi*, are addressed as *woi*.

Definition 9: *shu*. *Ji* and *woi* address the speaker as *shu* irrespective of sex

---

[1] cf. Radcliffe-Brown (1941), p. 11. This view has however, been disputed by Kroeber and others.

[2] A similar usage is common to nearly all non-Naga kinship systems in the Assam-Burma area. For some Naga variants on the same theme see Mills (1926), pp. 166, 169.

As long as the child remains at home, it needs no further extension of its kinship terminology; but as soon as the mother's parents are visited, a further group of relatives require classification. It follows from the argument of the last paragraph that the father's father and the mother's father must be covered by the same term. Hence, by Rule 6, it follows that *ji* and *woi* can be extended to all members of age groups senior to the mother, resident in the patrilocal group of the mother's father.

> *Definition 7—Extension*: *ji*. All males whom the mother addresses as *wa*, or *ji*, are addressed as *ji*.
> *Definition 8—Extension*: *woi*. All females whom the mother addresses as *nu*, or *woi*, are addressed as *woi*.

For simplicity, we will refer to the patrilocal group of the mother's father as 'the mother's group', and to the speaker's own patrilocal group as 'the speaker's group'.

The males of the mother's age group in the mother's group are important to a child of either sex. For the male child, these are in the class of potential wife's father (Hyp. 6, Rule 8). For the female child, they are in the class of males with whom sex relations are forbidden (Hyp. 7, Rule 7). According to Rule 5, the term *wa* cannot be extended to any males of the mother's group; similarly none of the other terms so far defined is appropriate. A new term is therefore needed:

> *Definition* 10: *tsa*. Males of the mother's group who belong to the mother's own age group are addressed as *tsa*.[1]

Among the females of the mother's group, the male child must distinguish between those who are marriageable and those who are unmarriageable. A woman may be unmarriageable because she is married already, or because she stands in a prohibited degree of relationship to the speaker. Hence:

> *Definition* 11: *ni*. A male addresses the wives of the males of the mother's group, other than *woi*, as *ni*.
> *Definition* 12: *rat*. A male child addresses the female children of the mother's group who are older than himself as *rat*.
> *Definition* 13: *nam*. A male addresses the women younger than himself who belong by birth to his mother's group as *nam*.

Since, by Hyp. 5, *rat* on reaching puberty become the wives of *hpu*, they are for the most part resident members of the speaker's own group.

The speaker (male) stands in a non-marriageable relationship to *ni* and *rat*, but in a marriageable relationship to *nam* (female). If the speaker

---

[1] If Rule 8 were omitted, the term *ji* might be extended to cover this group, in which case the corresponding reciprocals, *shu* and *hkri*, would also elide (see Def. 16). In several of the Naga and Chin systems, elision of this type does occur: see Shaw (1928), App. C; Mills (1937), pp. 128–37. See also the VaNdau variant of the Omaha type, mentioned by Radcliffe-Brown (1941), p. 13.

is by birth a member of B, then *nam* and *rat* were both born into C and *ni* into CC. If our B group child is female, this threefold classification is unnecessary. After marriage, the B group female child will reside in A, and will be remote from C and CC relatives. Hence:

Definition 14: *ning.* A female addresses all the female individuals whom her brother would address as *ni, rat,* or *nam,* as *ning.*

Initially, therefore, a female child does not use the terms *ni, rat* and *nam* at all. Later she will use *rat* towards males younger than herself (see Def. 12, Ext.), and *nam* towards members of the junior generation who are *nam* to her husband; but a female will never use the term *ni.*

The adult extension of the term *nam* follows from Rules 3 and 4:

Definition 13—*Extension A: nam.* An adult male addresses as *nam* the *hpu* and *nau* of all females of *age group junior to himself* whom he addresses as *nam* in accordance with Def. 13, above.

Definition 13—*Extension B: nam.* An adult female addresses as *nam* all those, of either sex, who would be addressed as *nam* by her husband, with the exception of females who are already *nau* to herself in accordance with Def. 6, above.

In the mother's group, there remain only the males of the speaker's own age group. For the female child these are covered by Hyp. 7 and Rule 7 (see Def. 10, above):

Definition 10—*Extension: tsa.* A female addresses all males (other than *ji*) in the mother's group as *tsa.*

This category will include even the males of age group junior to the speaker whom a male would address as *nam,* in accordance with Def. 13, Ext. A (above).

A male child first encounters the males of his own age in his mother's group as playmates. Their social attitude towards him is very similar to that of his *hpu-nau,* but the extension of the latter terms is excluded by Rule 5. The emphasis is strongly on equality of status, and the authority content of the term *tsa* (Def. 10, Rule 8) is inappropriate. A new term is therefore needed:

Definition 15: *hkau.* A male addresses all males in the mother's group, of the speaker's own age group, as *hkau.*

Reciprocals for the terms covered by Definitions 10–15 are now required. The equality of status emphasized by *hkau* is reciprocal:

Definition 15—*Extension: hkau.* A male addresses as *hkau* all males who would address the speaker as *hkau.*

Applying Rules 3 and 4, only one reciprocal is required for the terms *ni* and *tsa:*

Definition 16: *hkri*. Persons addressed as *ni* or *tsa* address the speaker of either sex as *hkri*.[1]

The term *rat* expresses a non-marriageable relationship between persons of the same age group. This condition is mutual:

Definition 12—*Extension*: *rat*. Persons addressed as *rat* address the speaker as *rat*.

The term *nam* (Def. 13) expresses primarily a marriageable relationship which is mutual. The term cannot, however, be made into its own reciprocal, since the sex of *nam* is indeterminate (Def. 13, Ext.) and its reciprocal use would lead to implications contrary to Hyp. 6 and 7. Moreover the male reciprocal of *nam* (female) is the class of potential husbands (Rule 8). Hence two reciprocals are required for the term *nam*, differentiating as to sex:

Definition 17: *gu*. Males who address persons of either sex as *nam* are themselves addressed as *gu*.

Definition 18: *moi*. Females who address persons of either sex as *nam* are themselves addressed as *moi*.

It may reasonably be objected that this is a highly artificial way of reaching the relationship with the father's sister, who is included in the class *moi*. Circumlocution seems, however, unavoidable, despite the fact that, according to Radcliffe-Brown (1941), the unity of the sibling group may be so firm that the father's sister can be regarded as 'a sort of female father' (p. 7). It must be remembered that the father's sister is here not a resident member of the child's own group; although biologically a close relative, sociologically she is somewhat remote. The basic unity here is the local group which, for the individual, is stratified into age groups or generations: this implies the unity of the sibling group (in Radcliffe-Brown's sense) in the case of children, but not in the case of adults. Kroeber and others have argued that place of residence may be a more fundamental social grouping than lineage descent, a contention borne out by this example.[2] Later we shall see that the term *moi* is extended in practice to cover wives of *gu* who are not blood relatives of the real father at all, which lends support to the rather artificial interpretation given here. [But see remarks at p. 29.]

[1] Initially *ni* is always the wife of *tsa*, who is of an age group senior to the speaker (Def. 10). But when the speaker is adult, the class *ni* includes the wives of *hkau* (mother's group) and of male *nam* (Def. 11). An adult male *hkri* may therefore be older than his *ni*. Similarly, an adult female *hkri* may be older than her *tsa* (Def. 10, Ext.).

[2] Kroeber (1938), p. 308 and *passim*. Compare also the careful distinction made by Radcliffe-Brown (1930) between the local group (horde) and its associated local clan among the Australian aborigines (p. 59, fn.). The importance of place of residence as a determinant of kinship category in Jinghpaw society evidently impressed early investigators. George (1891, p. xvi) asserts that an individual changes his/her clan affiliation with change of residence. This statement is incorrect, but is repeated by Wehrli (1904, p. 26) and others. See also the analysis by Gilhodes (1913, p. 363) of the *mayu-dama* relationship.

The term *ning* (Def. 14) covers primarily a wide group of unimportant relatives of the same sex. This unimportance is mutual:

Definition 14—*Extension*: *ning*. Females addressed as *ning* address the speaker as *ning*.

The eighteen terms thus defined (Def. 1–18) suffice to identify the kinship status of any two individuals within the hypothetical system composed of groups A, B, and C, since all needs are met by considering the relationship of the individual to members of his own and of his mother's group. We have studied, above, the relationship of a B group child to its own (B) group and to its mother's group (C). The B group child's relationship to members of its father's sister's husband's group (A) is analogous to the reciprocal relationship between a C group individual and the original B group child. The table of Reciprocal Terms (Table I) recapitulates the foregoing definitions.[1]

TABLE I. Reciprocal Terms

The terms in the two right-hand columns are the reciprocals of those in the two left-hand columns and vice versa.

SENIOR		JUNIOR	
Male	Female	Male	Female
Wa	Nu	Sha	Sha
Ji	Woi	Shu	Shu
Hpu	Na	Nau	Nau
Tsa	Ni	Hkri	Hkri
	Rat	Rat	
Gu	Moi	Nam	Nam
	Ning		Ning
Hkau		Hkau	

NOTE

In the *ni-hkri* relationship, the *hkri* is always male (Def. 14). In the *tsa-hkri* relationship, the *hkri* is male or female (Def. 10), and if female, unmarriageable (Hyp. 7).

[1] Rules 3 and 4 are expressly conditional. Our hypotheses have led to the following infringements of these rules:

(*a*) A man is in *tsa-hkri* relationship with his sister's daughters, but from Def. 14, Ext., his wife is in *ning-ning* relationship with the same females.

(*b*) Similarly, a woman is in *hkri-tsa* relationship with her brother's wife's brother's sons (Def. 10, Ext.), but in *ning-ning* relationship with her brother's wife's brother's daughters.

Under Def. 11, 12 and 13, we stressed that a male addressing females resident in his mother's group differentiates between married women (*ni*), unmarried women whom he cannot marry (*rat*), and marriageable women (*nam*). In the reciprocal situation, a female addressing the males of the father's sister's husband's group need differentiate only between marriageable (*gu*) and unmarriageable (*rat*), since, in view of Hyp. 4, married males must still be classed as marriageable (*gu*).

(*c*) *Hkau* (Def. 15), is a class of males of the same age group, which includes members both of the mother's group and of the father's sister's husband's group. This conflicts with Rule 8. In adult life, however, a *hkau* (mother's group) with marriageable daughters may turn into a *tsa*. [See also p. 29.]

D

While the use of these terms, in accordance with the definitions given, defines the relationship of any B group individual to all persons belonging to A and C groups, certain more remote individuals, belonging to groups AA and CC, are also relevant to the social context. We have already noted that *ni* is by birth a CC individual, in relation to a B speaker; it follows that the males of CC (i.e. the *hpu-nau of ni*) are also socially significant relatives. The child's approach to members of both C and CC groups is through its mother. From Def. 10, Ext., it follows that the mother of a B child addresses all males of CC either as *ji* or as *tsa*. If we compare these two terms as to affective tone, we see that the *ji-shu* relationship implies, *inter alia*, remoteness of relationship; in contrast, the *tsa-hkri* relationship has the specialized affect of constraint. Where *hkri* is female, it implies a sexual taboo; where *hkri* is male, it implies, among other attitudes, that of a son-in-law. It follows that *ji*, rather than *tsa*, is the appropriate term to extend to a category of affinal relatives chiefly characterized by remoteness of relationship:

Definition 7—Secondary Extension: *ji*. All males whom the speaker's mother would address either as *ji* or as *tsa* are addressed as *ji* by a speaker of either sex.

Reciprocally it follows that all persons of AA group, of either sex and any age, are *shu* to a male speaker of B. Thus, in logic, a whole clan is comprised under a single relationship term,[1] and if we insist upon translating terms, it would be formally correct to say that a Jinghpaw addresses his son's wife's brother's wife's brother as 'grandfather'. But translation of terms invites complicated explanations. I feel they are unnecessary. Diagrammatic analysis, on the other hand, by imputing equal weight to all parts of the diagram, tends to exaggerate the practical complexity. In our hypothetical system, for instance, the clan which is treated as a unity is also remote. Only one or two of these AA or CC relatives are ever likely to have dealings with a B group individual. In such circumstances, the undifferentiated classification of a whole clan grouping need not imply ambiguity. The principle of unification is, in fact, clearly the locality of residence, rather than lineage descent.

Table II reproduces our whole system in diagrammatic form. In each Local Group column, the terms on the left designate females, the terms on the right, males. The males have married, or will marry, the females

---

[1] Radcliffe-Brown (1941) describes this classification as being used 'to mark off a sort of marginal region between non-relatives and those close relatives towards whom specific duties and over whom specific rights are recognized' (p. 9). It should be distinguished from a unitary classification of nearer relatives such as that noted by Radcliffe-Brown for the matrilineal Cherokee (p. 13). But it is interesting to note that Radcliffe-Brown accepts the fact that 'the Cherokee were divided into seven matrilineal clans', for it has repeatedly been stated that the Jinghpaw are divided into five patrilineal clans. I will show, below, that this is a formal idealization which in no way corresponds with the present facts.

TABLE II. Diagram Illustrating Jinghpaw Relationship System

LOCAL GROUP	AA (SHU) Female	AA (SHU) Male	A DAMA Female	A DAMA Male	B HPU-NAU Female	B HPU-NAU Male	C MAYU Female	C MAYU Male	CC (JI) Female	CC (JI) Male
Age groups senior to parents'			HKRI / ning	GU / gu	MOI / moi	JI / ji	WOI / woi	JI / ji	WOI / voi	JI / ji
Parents' age group	SHU / ning	SHU / hkri	HKRI / ning	GU / gu	MOI / moi	WA / wa	NU / nu	TSA / tsa	NI / ning	JI / ji
Older than speaker	SHU / ning	SHU / hkri	HKRI / ning	HKAU / gu	NA / na	HPU / hpu	RAT / ning	HKAU / tsa	NI / ning	JI / ji
Speaker's own age group	SHU / ning	SHU / hkri	(madu va)		ego	EGO	(MADU ʒAN)			
Younger than speaker	SHU / ning	SHU / hkri	HKRI / ning	HKAU / rat	NAU / nau	NAU / nau	NAM / ning	HKAU / tsa	NI / ning	JI / ji
Son's age group	SHU / ning	SHU / hkri	HKRI / sha	HKRI / sha	SHA / nam	SHA / nam	NAM / ning	NAM / tsa	NI / ning	JI / ji
Age groups junior to son's	SHU / shu	SHU / shu	SHU / shu	SHU / shu	SHU / nam	SHU / nam	NAM / ning	NAM / tsa		

(The bracket spanning "Older than speaker", the ego row, and "Younger than speaker" is labelled "Speaker's own age group".)

in the column immediately to their right; they are the brothers (*hpu-nau*) of the females in the column immediately to their left; they are the sons (*sha*) of the males in the age-group level immediately above them; and they are the fathers (*wa*) of both the males and the females in the age-group level immediately below, in the same column. The central B group male is shown as 'EGO', his sister as 'ego' (representing the 'speaker' in the text above). In respect of each individual represented in the diagram, the term of address used by 'EGO' is shown in capital letters, and the corresponding term used by 'ego' is shown in lower case letters immediately below, thus: $\frac{RAT}{ning}$. The terms DAMA, HPU-NAU, MAYU, shown at the head of columns A, B, and C, are the Jinghpaw terms for these clan groupings, as used by both 'EGO' and 'ego' (see Section II). *Madu wa* and *Madu jan* signify 'husband' and 'wife', respectively.

In practice, the terms denoting affinal relationship are used in the same sense, whether or not all the marriages envisaged by the ideal system have actually taken place. Thus EGO's wife's father may not stand in any blood relationship to EGO's mother, but EGO's wife's father is nevertheless called *tsa*, EGO's wife's father's sister *nu*, EGO's wife's father's sister's husband *wa*, and so on. It is this type of adoptive relationship which makes the system appear unduly complicated when first encountered in the field.

In reading the diagram it should be understood that siblings of the same sex are always denoted by the same term, and that the children of siblings of the same sex are treated as siblings (Rules 5 and 6); thus the mother's sister is called *nu*, the mother's sister's husband *wa*, and the mother's sister's son (older than the speaker) *hpu*.

SECTION II: PRACTICE

The system of relationship terms described in Section I is the terminology actually employed by the Jinghpaw Kachins of North Burma. It has been described several times before[1]; but these earlier studies merely give lists, necessarily incomplete, of alternative translations of the different terms. In the field, these dictionary translations merely serve to make the practical application of the terminology seem more confusing than ever.

The various Jinghpaw dialects, including Gauri, Hkahku, Duleng, and Tsasen, appear to have systems structurally identical. Concerning Zi (Atsi), I am doubtful. The other Maru dialects, including Lashi, Nung, and Daru, although associated with a form of society very similar to that of the Jinghpaw, have systems which cannot be translated word for word into Jinghpaw, with identical extensions of meaning. I have therefore avoided the use of the rather vague term 'Kachin' in the title of this paper.

[1] By George (1891); Scott (1901); Hertz (1902); Wehrli (1904); Hanson (1906, 1913); Gilhodes (1922) and Hodson (1925).

The correspondence between the Jinghpaw reality and the hypothetical 'ideal' situation described in Section I is somewhat remote. The actual society is patrilineal; marriage is usually, but not always, patrilocal; the patrilineal lineage remains strictly exogamous for a few generations only; Hyp. 4 is valid; Hyp. 5 is an exaggeration (most girls are married before they are twenty, an elderly spinster is a great rarity); there is a marked preference for a man to marry into his *mayu*, but not necessarily into his mother's group (this distinction is explained below); the ban upon marriage between *hkri* and *tsa* is rigidly enforced only with respect to near relatives.

The normal Jinghpaw village (*gahtawng*) consists essentially of a single patrilineal-patrilocal group, even though the presence of ex-slaves and various affinal relatives may obscure the superficial picture. Larger settlements (*mareng*) consist of a number of such distinct *gahtawng*, grouped together on a kinship basis: that is to say, the component *gahtawng* are either distinct lineages of the same clan, or else lineages of different clans linked in *mayu-dama* affiliation. In the ritual organization of the *mareng* as a whole, the differentiation into component groups of *mayu ni*, *dami ni*, and *hpu-nau ni* is fundamental. Any marriage between *hkri* and *tsa* within the *mareng* is inconsistent with such a structure.[1] This fundamental structure is heavily obscured near Government Stations and Mission Centres, and also in certain areas, especially in the Bhamo District, where for administrative reasons the authorities have either forcibly altered the lay-out of house sites or else exerted strong official pressure to bring about the amalgamation of unrelated and even hostile *gahtawng*.

In Section I, terms such as 'clan' and 'lineage' were avoided as far as possible, and I have given no indication of the size of the idealized patri-lineal-patrilocal group. In the real society, there is no specific point at which the collateral group, comprising all the agnates of a common male ancestor, cease to regard themselves as forming an exogamous group. Lineage fission is, however, a normal feature of the society.

An important feature of Jinghpaw custom is that succession follows the rule of ultimogeniture. In the semi-historical past, this rule was clearly linked with a tradition of expansion whereby, before the death of a chief (or head of a lineage), his elder sons broke away from the parent locality to found new settlements of their own. On the other hand there were various pressures, political and economic, which made drastic expansion of this kind very difficult. The net result was (and is) a clan distribution pattern in which the patrilocal group, at any one time, consists of a few

---

[1] In the southern, sophisticated part of the Jinghpaw region, including the Bhamo and Northern Shan States areas, marriages between even closely related *hkri* and *tsa* are by no means rare; but in Hpalang (Bhamo area), a *mareng* which I studied in detail in 1939, such marriages were then still so inconvenient that the 'guilty' couple would normally move to some other settlement. In the more conservative North the rule is more effective.

households only, while the clan unit comprises a number of such patrilocal groups, distributed over a wide area and intermingled with the patrilocal groups of other clans. In general the clan-lineage grouping is somewhat more stable than the local grouping. In practice, therefore, the patrilineal-patrilocal groups referred to in Section I (i.e. persons who regard one another as *hpu-nau*) are not all to be found in one place; a man may be in *hpu-nau* relationship with the inhabitants of numerous different settlements.

There are, however, various degrees of this *hpu-nau* relationship. When a man speaks of his *hpu-nau ni* he means, as a rule, the members of a restricted lineage group, some five or six generations in 'depth', sharing a lineage name and maintaining among themselves a rigid rule of exogamy. As against these there are the *hpu-nau lawu-lahta* ('the brothers below and above'), who are the members of similar lineage groups which, together with his own, form a single, theoretically exogamous, major lineage or sub-clan.[1] Beyond this range, a man's fellow-clansmen, if they are not also members of his own sub-clan, are recognized as *hpu-nau* only in a vague sense; they are perhaps *anhteng amyu* ('our sort'), but the exogamy rule is quite nominal. If a marriage in breach of this rule occurs, the respective lineages cease to make any pretence of being *hpu-nau*, and realign themselves as *mayu-dama*.

An example will illustrate this point. The LAHTAW clan group is split up into a large number of principal segments or sub-clans, of which two are named KADAW and SANA. These two groups have in turn dispersed and split into a large number of smaller lineages, ranging in depth from three to eight generations. Among the lineages of KADAW are LAYAWNG, SHWE-MONG, and LASHU; among the lineages of SANA are DAGAN, HPAUYAM, and ALAM. Layawng Gam, a member of the LAYAWNG lineage, is *hpu-nau* to all other members of that lineage, and he is *hpu-nau lawu-lahta* to all members of the SHWEMONG, LASHU and other KADAW lineages. For the time being, at least, these KADAW lineages jointly form an exogamous group: that is to say, in 1943 Layawng Gam knew of no instance to the contrary. Similarly the SANA lineages jointly form an exogamous group, although in this case Layawng Gam was less sure of his facts, the total group being larger. In contrast, however, the LAYAWNG-KADAW lineage has for at least three generations been in *mayu-dama* (marriageable) relationship with the DAGAN-SANA lineage, despite the fact that both groups recognize their common LAHTAW ancestry. Layawng Gam therefore tends to refer to all SANA as his *mayu ni*, although inconsistently he may admit that all members of the LAHTAW clan are his *hpu-nau ni*. This type

---

[1] This use of the term 'major lineage' is not intended to be strictly comparable to that of Evans-Pritchard (1940), ch. v, and Fortes (1945), p. 31. The Jinghpaw system is of course of a segmenting type somewhat analogous to that of the Nuer and Tallensi, but my data are too crude to be submitted to such refinements of terminology.

of fission is of long standing and is not due to the disruptive processes of culture contact. I know of no specific rule which states the number of generations of collateral separation that are necessary before the fission becomes orthodox. In the case quoted, LAYAWNG and DAGAN have no common ancestor in the male line in the last eight generations; but I believe that four or five generations would usually be considered adequate separation.

Such dispersion and splitting of the local group in no way affects the suitability of the kinship terminology. That terminology is adapted in the first place to the use of the members of the biological family and their immediate relatives. The extension of the terms to include more remote relatives is a matter of social convenience, and practice may vary considerably between one family and another.[1]

Hypotheses 6 and 7 prescribe marriage between persons in *gu-nam* relationship. In the narrowest sense, this implies the marriage of a man to his mother's brother's daughter; more generally it simply means marriage to a girl from his *mayu ni*. In Section I we postulated that the *mayu ni* were a single specific clan group; in practice, clan fission leads to a different structure. Using the terminology of Section I, any particular B group is *mayu* to several different groups (A, A′, A″, etc.) and *dama* to several different groups (C, C′, C″, etc.). This permits a wide range of orthodox marriages, and all my data go to show that a high proportion of marriages are in fact orthodox in this sense, even in relatively sophisticated areas. In any case, even where the marriage is unorthodox, the marriage itself creates a *mayu-dama* relationship between the parent groups, which may persist into later generations. In theory the *mayu-dama* relationship between two lineage groups is a permanent relationship, persisting through many generations; in practice it may so persist, alternatively it may be represented by a single isolated marriage. Just as a man has degrees of *hpu-nau ni*, he has also degrees of *mayu ni* and *dama ni*, ranging from groups having long-standing traditional relationships with his own, to groups with whom only an isolated marriage has been contracted. Where any two households are brought into *mayu-dama* relationship by virtue of a marriage, all the individuals of the two households address one another as if all the marriages of the hypothetical system had taken place. For example, the wife of an elderly *gu* is always *moi*, and the husband of a *rat* is *hpu*. In any particular village, this form of adoptive relationship is bound to lead to a number of paradoxical inconsistencies; these are resolved individually, in accordance with social convenience, rather than

[1] For example, the kinship affiliations of chiefs are very much more extensive than those of commoners.

The pattern of Jinghpaw kinship terminology is not specifically related to the political structure. Two main forms of political structure occur, the *gumsa*, a hierarchy of chiefs, and the *gumlao*, a structure of 'independent' village headmen, but the kinship pattern is common to both. See Leach (1954).

by any fixed rule. Provided the ban on marriage between near *hkri* and *tsa* is not infringed,[1] the grouping of households into *hpu-nau*, *mayu*, and *dama* involves no straining of the terminology.[2]

Various cultural mechanisms exist which serve to maintain the continuity of the clan structure and to prevent too drastic a disregard of the ideal order. In aristocratic lineages, for example, certain religious powers rest always with the *uma du*, that is, with the putative successor in the direct line of ultimogeniture from the original founder of the sub-clan. This individual always continues to reside in the original ancestral home. A share of these powers can be obtained by the remote agnatic households of the same clan by means of a ritual purchase, but whenever fission occurs and the household splits, these powers lapse and must be purchased anew from the original source. Similarly, a man taking a wife from a group not established by precedent as being his *mayu* may have to pay forfeits all round, both to his own *mayu* and to the other *dama* of his new *mayu*. The details of such transactions vary greatly in different areas, and also according to the social status of the parties concerned; but the general principle can be stated that, while it is fully recognized that the ideal pattern of society is capable of modification, each fresh infringement of the formal rules will prove in some degree economically expensive. Since such sanctions have religious as well as economic motivations, they tend to fall into disuse in christianized areas. Where Christianity prevails, therefore, practice and theory deviate more widely than elsewhere.

Although there is no evidence that the hypothetical system of relationships was ever a practical reality, the ideal pattern is clearly formulated in Jinghpaw mythology. According to one story, the Jinghpaw originally consisted of five clans only. These five clans (usually listed as MARIP, MARAN, N'HKUM, LAHPAI, and LAHTAW), were in *mayu-dama* relationship, in the manner of the five groups AA, A, B, C, and CC in Section I. Since in the myth these were the only groups, the system there is circular, the CC (LAHTAW) group taking wives from the AA (MARIP) group. This story has been widely recorded[3] and apparently accepted as representing

---

[1] It is interesting that pre-marital intercourse between *hkri* and *tsa* is not a serious offence. A man and a woman, if strangers, presume themselves to be in this relationship, but so also do lovers who, in formal flirtatious poetry, invariably address one another as *hkri* and *tsa*. [See also p. 29.]

[2] Where there are alternative ways of reckoning relationship, the more intimate term in general prevails. Thus in Hpalang, a particular N'HKUM lineage was *dama* to MARAN-NMWI and *mayu* to MARAN-GUMYJE; schematically, therefore, GUMJYE should have been *ji* to NMWI; actually they deemed themselves *hpu-nau* on the basis of the clan linkage. For similar types of adjustment in Polynesia, see Firth (1936), pp. 266–7.

[3] The myth of the five clans can to-day be recorded in almost any part of the Kachin Hills. This diffusion may be recent and due to the influence of mission school teachers from the Bhamo area. George (1891), Scott (1901), Hertz (1902), Wehrli (1904), Hanson (1913), and Gilhodes (1922) all give the story as valid for 'the Kachins' as a whole, but it is really only autochthonous in the Bhamo area.

historical fact, of which the present practice is merely a decayed form: but I have found no justification for such an assumption. Jinghpaw mythical origins show no homogeneity; clan-origin myths are extremely numerous and mutually inconsistent, most of them being clearly linked with disputed rights to chieftainships and territory. In any case they mention a large number of 'original' clans additional to the five listed above. Moreover the ancestors whose marriages are thus mythically recorded seldom took their wives from the theoretically appropriate *mayu* group. The story can, however, be said to have a practical functional significance since it specifies an ideal society in which patrilineal clan groupings are arranged in *mayu-dama* relationships, and these relationships are permanent. Nevertheless, there is no reason to suppose that the Jinghpaw, as a whole, ever adhered in practice to the theoretical scheme.

On the other hand, examples do occur of 'small circles' (*hkauwang hku*, lit. 'first cousin circle path') in which three groups only (A, B, C) are in a circular marriage relationship to each other. In such cases the AA group coincides, from the terminological point of view, with the C group, and the CC group coincides with the A group. Presumably the wives of *mayu* males (male speaking) are still *ni* and not *hkri*, but I have no first-hand evidence of this. Such 'small circles' are entered into almost exclusively by aristocratic families,[1] and for the avowed purpose of political alliance and the conservation of the economic resources which would otherwise be dissipated by costly brideprice exchanges. There is a tendency for such arrangements to be reached by aristocratic (*du baw*) lineages within a single clan, which jointly own a consolidated block of clan territory. An example is the case of the three MARIP lineages UM, MASHAW, and N'DING which between them provide the principal chiefs in the Marip tracts in the North Triangle area. These lineages, which would normally have been in *lawu-lahta* relationship, are in fact linked by marriage: UM are *mayu* to MASHAW, who are *mayu* to N'DING, who are *mayu* to UM. The system has been stable for several generations, and were it not for the disturbing influence of the British administration it would, I gather, have been linked with a political arrangement whereby the paramount chief for the whole tract is provided by each group in turn. A similar arrangement prevails among some of the chiefs of the neighbouring Lahpai tracts.

The ban upon marriage between *rat* deserves comment. A *rat* (female) is normally a married woman; I doubt if this term would be applied to an unmarried woman unless she were very markedly older than the speaker. The levirate, in the form of the compulsory marriage of a younger brother with his elder brother's widow, has been reported.[2] Where the widow is

The story, in this form, does not fit the clan situation in the North. See Kawlu Ma Nawng (1943). [See Leach (1954), chapter ix.]

[1] However, Gilhodes (1913), records a similar practice among three commoner (*darat*) lineages, comprising the *mareng* of Matan in the Bhamo area (p. 375).

[2] See Anderson (1876), p. 142, and *Census of India* (1911), vol. ix, Burma, Pt. 1, p. 152. Gilhodes (1913, p. 375), however, confirms the view I express here.

elderly, such unions probably do not imply cohabitation, but an obligation certainly lies on a man's near *hpu-nau* relatives to care for his widow and children. The *rat-rat* relationship is I think usually unaffected by the death of the woman's husband. A young widow either becomes a wife of one of her other *gu* (from among her husband's *hpu-nau*), or else reverts to her own people, against repayment of the brideprice. In the latter case she would be free to remarry into any suitable group. [This is true only of the Gauri Kachins of the Bhamo area (see below p. 117).]

In Table II, the society is stratified horizontally by age groups, not by generations. The distinction is arbitrary except in the speaker's own patrilocal group, where the stratification is definitely by biological generation. Outside the local group, this may not be so. Old men may marry young girls as their second wives; a husband may then be as old as his wife's father, or older. The distinction between *hkau* and *tsa* here becomes somewhat indefinite.

In practice a distinction is made between real and classificatory parents. Usages vary locally. Gilhodes (1911, p. 883) gives a long list of distinguishing particles recorded in the Gauri area. In general usage are the terms below:

> *Wa di* for *wa* older than the real father
> *Wa doi* for *wa* younger than the real father
> *Nu tung* for *nu* older than the real mother
> *Nu doi* for *nu* younger than the real mother

By abbreviation, the particularizing particle may sometimes be used alone. Thus some observers have recorded *tung* as the term for the mother's elder sister, and *n'doi* as the term for the mother's younger sister. Similar particles, for use with *ji* and *woi*, are listed by Hanson (1906). The following variants fall into a rather different category:

(a) *In parts of Myitkyina District*

jum	....	....	....	.... father's father
ji	....	....	....	.... father's father's father

(b) *In the Bhamo and Northern Shan States Areas*

ji hkai	....	....	....	.... father's father
ji ke	....	....	....	.... father's father's father
ji dwi	....	....	....	.... mother's father
ji ke dwi	....	....	.... mother's father's father
woi hkai	....	....	.... father's mother
woi ke	....	....	....	.... father's father's mother
woi dwi	....	....	.... mother's mother
woi ke dwi (dwi ke)	....	.... mother's father's mother

But in contrast to the above are the terms Gilhodes (1911) gives for the Gauri:

hkai ji	....	....	....	....	mother's father
hkai woi		....	....	....	mother's mother
ji	....	....	....	....	father's father
woi	....	....	....	....	father's mother

The essential kinship category in all these phrases is *ji* (male), *woi* (female); the other particles merely provide sub-categories of these classes and should not be regarded as kinship terms in themselves, even if, by abbreviation, they may occasionally be used alone. In the Tsasen dialect the phrase *mayu-shayi* is used where I have used *mayu-dama*. Doubtless there are numerous other dialect variations.

To distinguish between two relatives of the same class the personal name is added, as in *Hpu Gam*, *Hpu Naw*. In the normal forms of address to equals or seniors, the relationship term is used and not the personal name: thus, '*Hpu E!*' (not '*Gam E!*'). On the other hand, parents speaking to their own children address them by their personal name, or nickname, rather than indiscriminately as *sha*. Husbands and wives usually address one another by their personal names. *Madu wa* may sometimes be used by a wife, but is formal; the reciprocal *madu jan* is a term of reference only. *Hpu ba*, *na ba* ('big brother', 'big sister') are common ways of distinguishing the eldest real brother and the eldest real sister, respectively.

Complete strangers are addressed by kinship terms of low affective content. The following are common verbal usages:

EGO (male) speaking: to old man, *wa di*; to male of own age, *hkau*; to child, *sha*; to old woman, *woi*; to adult woman of own age, or younger, *hkri*.

ego (female) speaking: to male of own age, *tsa*; to male much younger, *shu*; to child, *shu*; to any other female, *ning*.

The terminology applied to clan and lineage groupings has already been discussed, but it must be understood that the meanings of the native expressions are very flexible. *Anhteng amyu* ('our sort') usually refers to the largest group still deemed exogamous, but it is sometimes used to include the whole of the original clan which is now subdivided. Similarly it is impossible to give a precise definition of the *lawu-lahta ni*. In some contexts it covers a 'residual category' of relatives: those who are not in the speaker's own group, and yet not *mayu* and not *dama*. These categories are well brought out in the rhetorical phrase which represents simply a flowery way of saying, 'All we Jinghpaw':

> *Anhteng kahpu kanau ni*
> We elder younger brothers
>
> *Lawu lahta ni*
> Those below and above
>
> *Mayu dama ni*
> Affinal relatives
>
> *Jinghpaw ni yawng*
> Jinghpaws all!

The term *htinggaw ni* ('members of a household') implies the members of the household group still resident within the ancestral home, i.e. the limited extended family. The members of such a household usually have a distinctive household name, a new one being adopted by a local group which splits off to form a new settlement. Such recently split lineages may jointly be spoken of as being of one *dap* ('hearth'), although now resident in different places. The distinction in scale between an *amyu* name and a household name is shown in the following example. On enquiring the ancestry of a certain Lahtaw Singgyi, I was told: *Lahtaw-Sana amyu re, shi a htinggaw amying Hpauyam re* ('His *amyu* is Lahtaw-Sana; his household name is Hpauyam').

Other authorities have listed certain further terms which have found no place in my tabulation. *Yung* (*kayung*) is a politely honorific term of reference for a brother (*hpu* or *nau*), but is seldom used by males. *Jan* has the force of 'female', *wa* of 'male', in the following contexts: *nau jan*, a younger sister; *nau wa*, a younger brother; *madu jan*, a wife; *madu wa*, a husband. *Madu ni* are the owner-occupiers of a house, considered jointly. The sex of children is distinguished by prefixes: *la sha* or *shadang sha*, boy; *num sha* or *shayi sha*, girl. Colloquially a wife is *num*, but where this has the improper connotation of concubine, wife becomes *numsha*. Politely 'my wife' is *nye sha a kanu* (lit. 'the mother of my child'). *Ma* or *mang* signifies child in a general, non-kinship sense, but also is a kind of title for juniors, like the English 'master' or 'miss'; thus Layawng Gam might be called merely 'Ma Gam', especially when a child or young adult.

DISCUSSION

The inverted presentation of the two main sections of this paper was chosen in order to make it easy to see that the practice of the Jinghpaw is a modification of the formal simplicity of a theoretical scheme. Had the practice been described first, it would have been difficult to demonstrate that it had any formal shape at all. In the field, the actual use of Jinghpaw kinship terminology impressed me as highly complex, yet it must be, I argued, *from the users' point of view*, the simplest possible logical system consistent with the rules of the society. The classifications of our own kinship terminology appear to us 'logical', the classifications of such a system as the Jinghpaw appear at first sight fantastic; yet they are simple to the Jinghpaw. The problem was, therefore, to find the ideal frame of reference, in terms of which the vagaries of Jinghpaw usage could appear logical and simple.

I found that the use of individual terms was, as it were, secondary; the basic ideology was the grouping of relatives, or rather of the households of relatives, into the three categories *hpu-nau*, *mayu*, *dama*. In practice, as we have seen, these groupings are not necessarily permanent, but they 'ought' to be; any Jinghpaw will tell the inquirer that, despite the contrary evidence provided by his own genealogy. What then is the significance of this 'ought', the assertion that 'in the old days' the *mayu-dama* relationship was permanent? I suggest that it is simply the logical framework against which the Jinghpaw themselves conceptualize their own kinship system. Granted the uniqueness and permanence of the *mayu-dama* relationship, the whole kinship terminology falls into place as a consistent whole, in the manner demonstrated in Section I; without that assumption the classifications are chaotic. For the Jinghpaw, the idealization that the *mayu-dama* relationship is permanent and unique implies in effect my original seven hypotheses; and I suggest that the Jinghpaw child does in fact learn to classify its relatives on the basis of this simplification, and that in consequence its mental classifications are closely similar to my 'definitions'. I repeat once more, however, that this does not imply that the reality ever coincided with the idealization.

The result of 'simplification', as expressed in diagram form in Table II, may still appear somewhat complicated, but the practical situation is not. A Jinghpaw classes all his relatives by locality as *hpu-nau*, *mayu* and *dama*, with the *ji ni* and *shu ni* as remote and little mentioned appendages of the last two categories. Indeed the term *ji ni* is most frequently used as an expression for the ancestors in the speaker's own lineage; if the phrase refers instead to the *mayu ni* of the *mayu ni*, the context makes this obvious. Thus if a man announces his intention to visit his *ji ni*, one can presume that he is not contemplating a visit to Hades! To arrive at the specific relationship within the major grouping involves no special feat of memory.

Turning to general theory, it is of interest to reflect that the system I have described might have been approached from several different viewpoints, with differing results. Historical reconstruction could find evidence of a five-clan structure and submerged matriliny in a patrilineal state; linguistic analysis would place the form of the term-diagram in a particular category, such as Lowie's 'bifurcate merging' type; structural analysis would arrive at structural principles similar, in part at least, to my structural rules. I hold, however, that the type of structural analysis favoured by Radcliffe-Brown postulates a formal rigidity which is not found in practice, so that it is always necessary to consider carefully in what sense these formal simplifications are a reflection of actual behaviour. In my treatment, I have stressed the distinction between the ideal and the normal pattern of behaviour. I suggest that the kinship terminology bears a specific relationship to an idealized form of the social order, but that there is no such obvious relationship between the kinship terminology and the social order as manifested in actual behaviour.

The system of kinship terminology displays the categories into which the speaker divides the individuals with whom he has social contact; in that sense there is a functional relationship between the use of a term and the behaviour adopted towards a particular individual. But this is a tenuous relationship. In the Jinghpaw system, the mother's brother and the wife's father fall into the same term category. Undoubtedly in certain contexts these two individuals fulfil somewhat similar ritual roles, but that is as far as the identity goes, and that link is not sufficient in itself to explain the kinship classification. This classification is, on the other hand, immediately understandable in terms of the idealization that the *mayu-dama* relationship should be both permanent and unique.

I must confess that I started this paper simply in a spirit of curiosity, to discover whether it was possible to deduce from 'first principles' a system which in the field had caused me many hours of exasperation. I am not suggesting that the result has yielded anything very original with regard to basic principles of structure, but I find it interesting that, after I had made the initial assumptions that differentiation would be on the basis of age and sex, and that simplicity should always prevail (that is, that the number of differentiated kinship categories should always be minimal), it proved possible to start with a highly simplified pattern of a society, and then deduce the categories of kinship terminology actually employed in the same society. In the process, a number of structural principles which have previously been enunciated by Radcliffe-Brown, Lowie, Kroeber and others have come to the surface. This probably means no more than that these principles are implied in the simplified pattern provided by the initial hypotheses. There is, however, one point which I would like to stress. I assume with Radcliffe-Brown that when individuals are comprised within a single kinship 'class', there is a principle of unification underlying that classification which can be discerned from an analysis of the social system. But I would contrast two types of unification. On the one hand, individuals are classed together because, individually and as a group, they stand in a significant and important relationship to the speaker; but on the other hand they may be classed together precisely because they are unimportant and remote. In the Jinghpaw system, *rat* is a class resulting from the first type of unification; *ning* a class resulting from the second. The same term may even comprise different groups of individuals, and express different principles of unification at different stages of life. To a woman speaker during her youth the term *tsa* signifies sexual constraint and where used in a strict kinship sense it is limited to age-group seniors of the *mayu* group with whom she has much social contact. In later life it comprises *all* males of the *mayu* group, including those younger than herself, this being a group with whom she now has little social contact.

Despite the abstraction, my treatment, while omitting the documentary detail of a normal intensive study, follows what Malinowski has called the 'biographical approach', that is, the development of kinship terminology as it is used from childhood to old age. This treatment brings out clearly two points which have been frequently stressed before: first, that the extensions of a classificatory kinship system are merely elaborations and modifications of simple childhood sentiments developed in the normal context of home life; and secondly, that although a classificatory system includes, in theory, an unlimited number of individuals, the practical number of persons involved is quite small, and in no case so large as to lead to ambiguity. [But see p. 28.]

Finally there is the question of the functioning of kinship terminology in conditions of social change. I have pointed out that if marriages between closely related *hkri* and *tsa* came to be generally recognized as correct, then the structural shape of the community, by which I mean the relationship of the kinship pattern to the local group pattern, would be radically altered. I have also mentioned that such marriages already occur, even if they are not yet regarded as orthodox. It follows, therefore, that ultimately there must come a stage where the divergence between practice and ideal is so great that there is a basic inconsistency; this must result in a terminological regrouping and a reconstruction of the ideal pattern. Such a prospect suggests a useful basis for attempting a comparative analysis of other societies in the Assam-Burma area, in which the same asymmetrical marriage rules are theoretically maintained, while other structural features differ.

The secondary extension of the *ji-shu* relationship has not previously been recorded explicitly, although it is implied by Hanson (1913), who gives *shu* as including 'sister's children's (*hkri ni a*) husbands and children'. This lack of previous observation may be accounted for by the fact that the brothers of *ni* are in any case remote relatives, while in many practical instances the use of *ji* to denote collaterals is avoided by the substitution of a closer relationship.

3

The Structural Implications of Matrilateral Cross-Cousin Marriage

INTRODUCTORY NOTE

SINCE the first appearance of this essay in 1951 its theme has been the subject of a good deal of academic discussion and the reader may find it useful to refer to a number of the following publications. Homans and Schneider (1955) in their critique of Lévi-Strauss (1949) dismiss my material as exceptional. Instead they claim to demonstrate by statistical means that matrilateral cross-cousin marriage is linked with the existence of paternal authority in a patrilineal structure while patrilateral cross-cousin marriage is similarly linked with avuncular authority in a matrilineal structure. I do not myself find their argument at all persuasive. As against this Needham (1958b) claims to have demonstrated that a rule of prescriptive patrilateral cross-cousin marriage is an impossibility. Powell (1956) and Leach (1958) have shown that Malinowski's evidence on this point, by which Homans and Schneider set great store, is defective. Trobrianders very seldom marry their father's sister's daughter. Vroklage (1952), in his account of Belu, provides an example of a matrilineal society practising Kachin type marriage in association with a structure of political hierarchy comparable to that recorded for the patrilineal Kachin, Lakher and Batak. Nakane (1958) has elaborated a suggestion given in the body of this essay (p. 57) and shown that certain sections of the Garo engage in what she calls a 'matrilineal Murngin' system of marriage. Needham (1958a) has re-examined the available evidence concerning the marriage practices of the Purum (p. 73) and reached conclusions somewhat different from mine.

Salisbury (1956) has sought to apply some of the ideas in this essay to a New Guinea context; in my view however, his use of the notion of asymmetrical marriage is unfortunate (Leach, 1957).

Following Kulp, Granet, Fei, and Hsu my essay devotes a good deal of space to the discussion of matrilateral cross-cousin marriage among the Chinese. Freedman (1958) has quite rightly pointed out that the empirical evidence for such marriage practices is very thin. There is no evidence that Chinese local descent groups ever intermarry systematically and asymmetrically on a regular 'wife-giving/wife-receiving' basis; all that has been recorded is that, in some areas, cross-cousin marriage is quite common and that in such circumstances marriage with the matrilateral cross-cousin is preferred not prescribed.

In the original essay (pp. 70, 72) I indicated that a full understanding of the Murngin system of marriage regulation would be impossible without additional information concerning the pattern of local grouping and the organization of trade. Since then Professors Elkin and Berndt have published a good deal of additional information concerning the Murngin area but many essential facts remain obscure (Elkin, 1953; Elkin and Berndt, 1951; Berndt, 1955 and 1957).

In the body of the essay (p. 73) my review of the earlier literature of 'Kachin type' marriage gives insufficient credit to the studies of Dutch scholars of systems of 'circulating connubium' in Indonesia. Fischer's contribution was certainly more influential than is suggested here, and it now seems likely that Granet's ideas were derived from Van Wouden rather than from Radcliffe-Brown.

*   *   *   *   *

Introduction

At first glance the theme of this essay might seem excessively narrow and pedantic; in fact, as I hope to show, it is very appropriate to the terms of the Curl Bequest competition. Firstly it is a topic that lies at the very heart of anthropological kinship theory. Secondly it is a branch of kinship theory to which a number of significant, and perhaps very important, contributions have been made during the past ten years. Thirdly it is a field to which I myself, from my own experience, can make a new and original contribution.

The essay is arranged in four sections.

Part 1—serves to establish certain basic definitions, assumptions and theoretical objectives.

Part 2—reviews the literature of the theme under discussion.

Part 3—provides material from my own fieldwork, and examines the relevance of this new material for the analysis of two other well documented societies which have not previously been considered from quite this point of view.

Part 4—summarizes the conclusions that may be drawn from this review of theory and ethnographic fact, and specifies a series of propositions, which not only accord with the facts as now known, but which are in a form which permits of further empirical testing in the field.

E

PART I

Basic Assumptions and Special Concepts

LOCAL DESCENT GROUPS

There are two kinds of marriage. The first results from the whims of two persons acting as private individuals; the second is a systematically organized affair which forms part of a series of contractual obligations between two social groups. When I mention an institutionalized or 'type' form of marriage, it is to this latter kind of arrangement that I refer.

In my view the social groups which 'arrange' such a marriage between themselves are, in almost all societies, of essentially the same kind. The core of such a group is composed of the adult *males* of a kin group all resident in one place. By this I do not mean to argue that women have no part to play in the arrangement of a marriage or that remotely situated kinsfolk are wholly ignored; I merely mean that the corporate group of persons who have the most decisive say in bringing about an arranged marriage is always a group of co-resident males representing, as a rule, three genealogical generations, namely: the old men or grandfathers, the normal adults or fathers, and the young adults or sons.

In practice, membership of such groups is defined by descent as well as residence. In this essay I am concerned only with systems of unilateral (and double unilateral) descent so that I can formulate the above proposition as follows:

In a unilaterally defined descent system where a clan or large scale lineage, ceases, for one reason or another, to be a localized group, then, in general, it ceases to be a corporate unit for the purposes of arranging a marriage. The corporate group which does arrange a marriage is, in such circumstances, always a group of males who, besides being members of the same lineage or clan, share a common place of residence.

In this essay I shall refer to corporate groups of this kind as *local descent groups*, or more simply, wherever the context is unambiguous, simply as 'groups'.

Logically speaking *local descent groups* thus defined can come about only in a limited number of ways. The following would appear to be the most likely possibilities:

(*a*) with patrilineal descent and patrilocal residence.

(*b*) with matrilineal descent and 'avuncolocal'[1] residence (i.e., residence in the community of the mother's brother), succession to male authority being from mother's brother to sister's son.[2]

---

[1] This term has been proposed by Murdock (1949, p. 17).

[2] The normal Trobriand rule; Malinowski (1932a, pp. 10, 83). A man moves to his mother's brother's village when adolescent and then brings his wife to join him in that village; cf. the Congo Mayombe system as analysed by Richards (1951).

(c) with matrilineal descent and 'matrilocal' residence (i.e., residence in the community of the wife) coupled with matrilateral cross-cousin marriage (father's sister's son—mother's brother's daughter); succession to male authority being from father-in-law to son-in-law.[1]

DIAGRAM LINES: LOCAL LINES AND DESCENT LINES

Figs. 4, 5a and 5b illustrate diagrammatically the notion of *local descent groups* as resulting from each of the above situations. In this essay I shall refer to such diagrammatic local descent groups as *local lines*. Thus in these figures the lines A_1–A_2–A_3; B_1–B_2–B_3; C_1–C_2–C_3 each represent *local lines*. The kinship relation between any two individuals in such a diagram is always intended to be classificatory rather than actual; thus A_2 is classificatory son of A_1: B_2 is classificatory sister's son to B_1.

This notion of a *local line* is to be distinguished from the parallel concept of a *descent line* ('line of descent') which has frequently been used by Radcliffe-Brown and his pupils. Descent lines have nothing whatever to do with local grouping, they are merely a diagrammatic device for displaying the categories of the kinship system in relation to a central individual called Ego. The number of basic descent lines in such a diagram depends merely upon how many different kinds of relative are recognized in the grandfather's generation. It has nothing to do with the number of local descent groups existing in the society.[2]

Failure to distinguish between the notion of local line (indicating a local descent group) and descent line (indicating a set of kinship categories) has been the source of much confusion.

One particularly important difference between these two types of diagram is this: A *descent line* commonly comprises at least five generations, e.g. grandfather, father, Ego, son, grandson and each of these individuals is given equal weight. A *local line* on the other hand seldom contains more than three generations at any one time.[3] As a child, Ego is a member of a system comprising the local descent groups of which his parents and grandparents were members by birth; as an adult, Ego is a member of a system comprising the local descent groups of himself and his wife and

---

[1] The Garo pattern. Hodson (1921); Bose (1936). The Bemba and Yao systems appear to be partly, if not consistently, of this type; cf. Richards (1951).

Of the other logical alternatives, consistently patrilineal-matrilocal societies do not, I think, occur. Matrilineal-patrilocal societies are reported but are probably 'ethnographic errors' in that these are really either cases of double descent or else not consistently patrilocal. The Ila and Ashanti, for example, have both at times been described as matrilineal-patrilocal, but in both societies there is an element of double descent while the Ashanti have no 'normal' pattern of residence; cf. Richards (1951) on the Ila, Fortes (1949, 1950) on the Ashanti. Cf. also de Josselin de Jong (1951), p. 190.

[2] See Radcliffe-Brown (1951, p. 43).

[3] A man may have classificatory grandfathers and classificatory grandchildren alive at the same moment, but it is not likely that they will both be members of Ego's own local group.

the local descent groups into which his children are married. These two systems of kinship association overlap but do not normally both exist in their totality at one and the same time. Ego's father and grandfather and

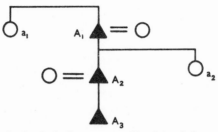

FIG. 4.—The line A_1–A_2–A_3 indicates a patrilineal local descent group resulting from patrilocal residence.

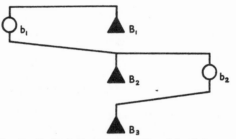

FIG. 5a.—The line B_1–B_2–B_3 indicates a matrilineal local descent group resulting from avuncolocal residence.

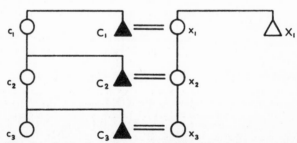

FIG. 5b.—The line C_1–C_2–C_3 indicates a matrilineal local descent group resulting from matrilocal residence and matrilateral cross-cousin marriage.

In this system C_2 succeeds C_1 because he is husband of x_2 and potential husband of x_1. Only with matrilateral cross-cousin marriage are C_1 and C_2 of the same descent group.

their contemporaries are mostly dead before Ego's grandchildren are born. A diagram designed to show *descent lines* instead of *local lines* tends to obscure this very important fact.

TYPE MARRIAGES

Readers of this essay will be familiar with the notion of type marriages which has been developed by Radcliffe-Brown to describe the various forms of institutionalized marriage regulation found among Australian tribes (Radcliffe-Brown, 1930, *passim*; 1951, pp. 41–42). Type marriages form a very convenient shorthand notation and in this essay I shall employ the following series:

1. *Kariera type*—'symmetrical cross-cousin marriage'. This system approves the simultaneous or nearly simultaneous exchange of women between two local descent groups. In the ideal type a man marries the mother's brother's daughter who is sister to his own sister's husband.

I am not concerned with the other Australian symmetrical type marriages but it may be noted that the Aranda type, and the Kumbaingeri type, both approve marriage with the sister of a man's own sister's husband. They differ from the Kariera type only in excluding from marriage certain categories of women who would be admissible as 'mother's brother's daughter/ father's sister's daughter' in the Kariera system of kinship.[1]

2. *Trobriand type*—'asymmetrical cross-cousin marriage (patrilateral)'. This system precludes the reciprocal marriage of a man with the sister of his own sister's husband, but it amounts nevertheless to a systematic exchange of women between two local descent groups. The exchange is completed only after a time lag of one generation. In the ideal type a man marries the father's sister's daughter; he is forbidden to marry the mother's brother's daughter.

This kind of marriage regulation occurs in patrilineal as well as matrilineal societies. I shall use the description *Trobriand type marriage* in both cases.

3. *Kachin type*—'asymmetrical cross-cousin marriage (matrilateral)'. This system precludes altogether the exchange of women between two local descent groups. If group B gives a woman to group A, the service is never reciprocated in kind, though it may of course be reciprocated in other ways—e.g., by marriage payments. In the ideal type a man marries the mother's brother's daughter; he is forbidden to marry the father's sister's daughter.

My Kachin type includes the Australian Karadjeri type and thus includes the much discussed Murngin system. It should be noted however that, in general, Kachin type systems lack those features of the Karadjeri type which make the latter characteristically Australian—e.g., the formal division of the local descent group into sections composed of alternating generations (Radcliffe-Brown, 1951, pp, 43, 55).[2]

[In the terminology used by Needham (1958b) these type marriages all reflect prescriptive rules, not marriage preferences: the individual is required to choose a mate from a single specifically named category of kin.]

[1] The same can be said of the somewhat anomalous Ambryn system (Deacon, 1927, pp. 328–9; Seligman, 1927, p. 374.)

[2] It is worth noting that the South Indian regulation described by Aiyappan which forbids marriage with F.sis.d. but approves marriage with both m.B.d. and own sister's daughter is *not* a case of Kachin type marriage as it can result in

ASSUMPTIONS AND OBJECTIVES

For the purposes of this essay I assume that the three varieties of cross-cousin marriage defined above, the Kariera type, the Trobriand type and the Kachin type, can usefully, for purposes of comparison, be treated as institutional isolates. I am interested in the implications of such institutionalized behaviour for the societies in which such rules occur.

The total literature on the subject of cross-cousin marriage is very large; the major part of it has been recently reviewed by Lévi-Strauss (1949). In this essay I am primarily concerned only with that part of this material which deals with Kachin type marriage; I shall concern myself with Kariera and Trobriand type marriages only so far as is necessary to provide contrasts and comparisons.

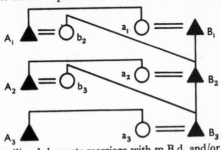

FIG. 6.—Patrilineal descent; marriage with m.B.d. and/or own sis.d.

The particular aspect of Kachin type marriage which interests me is this. Where such a system of institutionalized marriage rules exists in association with local descent groups, then a group B which provides wives for group A is not compensated in kind. There are then three possibilities:

(1) That the principle of reciprocity does not apply at all and that group B obtains no compensation;

(2) that reciprocity is achieved by group A giving group B some form of economic or political compensation—e.g., marriage payments, work service, political fealty;

(3) that three or more groups, A, B, C, make mutual arrangements to 'marry in a circle'—C giving wives to B, who give wives to A, who give wives to C again. In this case the wives that C gives to B are, in a sense, compensation for the wives that B gives to A.

The implications of these alternative possibilities form the subject matter of this essay.

But let me be quite clear about what I mean by *implication*. I am not concerned with the origins of institutional rules. It seems to me probable that such marriage rules as we are discussing may have originated in quite an exchange of women between groups. See Fig. 6. a_2 and b_3 are both simultaneously m.B.d. and sis.d. to their respective husbands B_2 and A_2. (Cf. Aiyappan, 1934.)

different ways in different societies. I am also not greatly interested in
what Malinowski might have called the overt function of such behaviour.
I have no doubt that in different societies one and the same rule will
serve different immediate ends; comparison in terms of such ends can
therefore only lead to purely negative results.[1] What I am interested in
however is the 'function' of such rules in a mathematical sense. For
example: Given a rule such as that which defines Kachin type marriage,
and given various other common elements between society A and society
B, can we infer, by logical arguments, that some other unknown characteristic 'x' must also be common to our two societies? And if we think we
can do this, how far do empirical facts justify such a claim?

DIAGRAMS

In my discussion of the literature in the later sections of this essay it will
become apparent that serious misunderstandings have constantly arisen
from a tendency to confuse structural diagrams with ethnographic reality.[2]
In my own argument I shall constantly refer to diagrams such as those of
Figs. 7 and 8. It is important that the reader should clearly understand
just how these diagrams relate to reality.

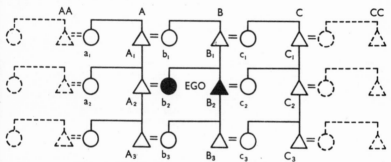

FIG. 7.—Kachin type marriage system (patrilineal).
Lines A, B, and C alone can be thought of as *local lines*. If the whole scheme be
considered including lines AA and CC then the vertical lines are *descent lines* (see
text).

In a system of unilineal descent, either patrilineal or matrilineal,
Kachin type marriage has the effect of grouping Ego's relatives into at
least three mutually exclusive categories, namely:

A. Groups containing 'father's sister's daughters'.
B. Groups containing 'sisters'.
C. Groups containing 'mother's brother's daughters'.
Ego (male) is permitted to marry only into groups C.
Ego (female) is permitted to marry only into groups A.

[1] This I think is clearly shown by Hsu (1945).
[2] Cf. Radcliffe-Brown (1951, *passim*) for criticism of Lawrence and Murdock
on this score.

With Trobriand type marriage, on the other hand, a group which contains a father's sister's daughter in one generation will contain a mother's brother's daughter in the next.[1] There is thus no category of local descent groups which are 'non-marriageable' for Ego (male) although outside his own clan.

This distinction between Kachin type and Trobriand type is made clear in Figs. 7 and 8. In Fig. 7 the three lines, A, B, C, can be taken to represent three patrilineal local descent groups intermarrying according to Kachin type marriage. In Fig. 8 the three lines, A', B', C', can be taken to represent three matrilineal local descent groups intermarrying according to Trobriand type marriage. In the first case the relationship of group B to group A and of group B to group C is quite distinct. B receives wives from C and gives wives to A. In the second case the general type of relationship between B' and A' is the same as that which exists between B' and C', but merely shifted one generation. This argument first appears clearly stated in Fortune (1933).

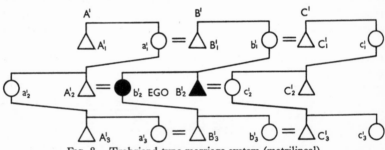

FIG. 8.—Trobriand type marriage system (matrilineal).
Lines A', B', C' can be thought of as *local lines*.

In Kachin type systems the division of Ego's relatives into three mutually exclusive categories is a minimum; there may be further categories of a like kind. In theory for example it might seem, as in Fig. 7, that there must always be a further group AA related to A in the same way as A is related to B, and that there must always be a group CC related to C in the same way as C is related to B.

If we are merely seeking to display the categories of the kinship system by a diagram of *descent lines*, it is very probable that these extra lines AA and CC will be necessary. In the actual Kachin system this is the case (Leach, 1945), and also in the Australian Yir-Yoront system (Sharp, 1934). The much discussed Murngin system requires in all no less than 7 lines (Warner, 1930–31), so that the diagram contains further lines AAA and CCC to the left and right respectively.

But this wide extension of the descent line diagram does not necessarily

[1] E.g., in Fig. 8 c_2' is father's sister's daughter to B_2' but c_3' is mother's brother's daughter to B_3'.

imply that an equal number of *local descent groups* are associated with Ego's own group. If Fig. 7 denotes *local lines* (local descent groups) instead of *descent lines* then there is no reason why AA should not coincide or at any rate overlap with B. This is the crux of Murdock's and Lévi-Strauss's misunderstanding of the Murngin system which has been criticized by Radcliffe-Brown (1951).[1]

If we are concerned with *descent lines* it is always true that the most satisfactory diagram model which will represent the whole of a Kachin type marriage system will consist of some uneven number of lines, Ego's own line being centrally placed. In contrast, any system of marriage regulations which approves the marriage of a man with his sister's husband's sister (e.g. Kariera, Aranda, Ambryn types) can be most easily represented by a diagram model containing an even number of lines, Ego's own position being immaterial. This fact also has led to much confusion.

In Fig. 7 the central part, lines A, B, C, can be taken as a diagram of *local lines*; but the full scheme, including lines AA and CC, can only be a diagram of *descent lines*—it merely shows the categories into which Ego's relatives necessarily fall. It says nothing at all about the totality of Ego's society. That total society may contain any number of local descent groups; Fig. 7 only specifies three of them, namely, A, B, and C; the remainder might potentially fit in anywhere. For instance, suppose there is a local descent group X to which B is either unrelated, or only remotely related; then if Ego (male) marries a woman of X, X will thereafter be rated as category C—'wife giving'; but if Ego (female) marries a man of X, X will thereafter be rated as category A—'wife taking'.

The majority of writers who have discussed Kachin type marriage systems have failed to understand this. Instead they have been led to assume that a diagram such as Fig. 7 can serve to represent not merely the whole kinship system, but the whole of Ego's society. Once this assumption is made certain erroneous inferences appear to follow immediately. In the first place if lines AA and CC denote local descent groups, then AA has no husbands and CC has no wives; it must then follow that CC take wives from AA. The system then becomes circular. Furthermore the five lines, AA, A, B, C, CC, now cease to denote merely categories of Ego's relatives, they become actual segments of the total society, and can be thought of as 'marriage classes', or perhaps as five strictly exogamous phratries which by some mystical process always manage to remain of exactly equal size and sex composition.

Radcliffe-Brown (1951, *passim*) has rightly criticized Murdock's analysis of the Murngin system on this score; I shall likewise criticize the work of Hodson, Mrs Seligman, Granet, Lévi-Strauss and others. But I would like to make it clear that the problem at issue is not simply one of understanding the ethnographic facts. In a number of societies which possess Kachin type marriage systems the native informants themselves habitually

[1] See also p. 69.

explain the intricacies of their kinship system by saying that the society consists of 3 or 5 or 7 clans which 'marry in a circle', and it requires the collection of genealogies to prove that this description is a fiction. Furthermore, cases can be found where three or more local descent groups do in fact, as well as in theory, 'marry in a circle' on a continuous and more or less exclusive basis. The correspondences as well as the contradictions between ideal model and empirical fact therefore call for comment and analysis.

PART 2

The literature on Kachin Type Marriage 1920-1951

EARLY THEORIES

Before I come to my own analysis of these problems I must review the literature in which this type of institutionalized behaviour has previously been discussed; for I recognize that the theories of 1950 are only elaborations of the theories of 1920 and 1930. If my comments seem almost uniformly adverse, it is partly for the following reason. The writers whom I am about to mention have all in one way or another propounded theories about 'cross-cousin marriage', but they have done so with sundry different ends in view. Some have been interested in the origins of human society, some in the algebra of kinship terminology, some in asserting dogmatically some principle of ethnographic cause and effect, and some again simply in denying such assertions. Only one of them, it seems to me, namely, Professor Lévi-Strauss, has developed his theory in the spirit of logical deduction and demonstration which I have outlined above as my own objective. That being so I am often in sympathy with the views of Professor Lévi-Strauss because I think I understand what he is trying to do; likewise I am often out of sympathy with other writers merely because I do not understand what they are trying to do.

In Part 1 we have seen not only that there are three distinct types of cross-cousin marriage but that each of these types has quite different structural implications. Although the significant literature on 'cross-cousin marriage' extends back at least to the early years of this century (Rivers, 1907) the clear appreciation of the importance of these distinctions is a relatively late development. Frazer, Westermarck and others had indeed, before 1920 (Frazer, 1918, vol. 2, pp. 98ff.), noted the widespread occurrence of asymmetrical cross-cousin marriage of both varieties, but these phenomena were not then generally regarded as separate isolates distinct from reciprocal cross-cousin marriage.[1] As late as 1929 in an *Encyclopaedia Britannica* article entitled 'Cousin Marriage' Miss Wedg-

---

[1] Rivers (1921) however stresses that 'we need evidence not only concerning the exact distribution of the three varieties, but also . . . we need to know with what other practices each form of marriage is associated'.

wood (1929) (clearly under the aegis of Malinowski) confuses all three types of cross-cousin marriage, and merely takes note of the occurrence of the Kachin type 'in a tribe in Assam'. Malinowski's dogmatism was perhaps partly responsible for this lack of discrimination. In the heyday of functionalism simple cause and effect relationships were all that were sought for in the way of explanation for structural phenomena. If an institutionalized arrangement could be shown to 'satisfy a need', it was not considered necessary to look further. In the Trobriands, a man's heir is his sister's son. As can be seen from Fig. 8, with Trobriand marriage the sister's son of a sister's son is Ego's own grandson (son's son) and he will marry Ego's own granddaughter (daughter's daughter); thus this type of marriage serves to conserve property titles in the patrilineal line in defiance of matrilineal inheritance and descent.[1] This led Malinowski (1932, p. 86) to assert that, in the Trobriands, such marriage 'is undoubtedly a compromise between two ill adjusted principles of mother right and father right; and this is its main *raison d'être*'. Miss Wedgwood (1929) went much further and asserted of cross-cousin marriage in general that 'its most important effect is on the transmission of property'.[2]

At the date of Miss Wedgwood's article Kachin type marriage had already been treated as an independent isolate by one or two writers. The earliest of these appears to have been Gifford (1916) in his study of the Miwok. Gifford seems to have been mainly interested in the correlation between marriage rule and kinship terminology. In the fashion of his day, after the model of Rivers, he perceived the system as one of secondary marriages. His own summary of the argument is:

'The right of a man to marry his wife's brother's daughter was relegated to his son, who thus married his father's wife's brother's daughter, in other words his own cross-cousin (mother's brother's daughter)' (Gifford, 1922, p. 256).

Gifford does not appear to have recognized that such an arrangement would imply a special continuing relationship between the 'wife taking lineage' on the one hand and the 'wife giving lineage' on the other.

The papers published in the decade 1920–30 which seem to have had the greatest influence upon subsequent theory are those by Hodson (1921–5), Mrs Seligman (1928), and Warner (1930).

---

[1] In terms of Fig. 8 B_3' who is the second generation heir to B_1''s land titles is son's son to B_1' and will marry a_3' who is daughter's daughter to the same man. This of course assumes marriage to the real rather than classificatory father's sister's daughter. [The empirical facts seem to be that Trobrianders seldom marry the true father's sister's daughter.]

[2] This type of functional explanation of cross-cousin marriage was first made by Hill-Tout (1907, p. 145) and was argued in greater detail by Richards (1914). The argument may of course be perfectly valid in some cases. In the Trobriands for example only a minority of marriages are 'arranged' at all and these are usually in households such as those of chiefs which possess substantial inheritable property.

It was Hodson who seems to have been the first to recognize that while Kariera type marriage can be operated by, at a minimum, two exogamous groups, Kachin type marriage involves at least three such groups.[1] He seems therefore to have advocated a classification of Assam tribes into those with dual organization and those with tripartite organization,[2] corresponding to the type of cross-cousin marriage adopted. Hodson found in the Kachins an ideal example of the latter kind of organization. He assumes this society to consist of five exogamous 'divisions' marrying in a circle. All the ethnographers have made it clear that the Kachins do not in fact adhere at all closely to their own theoretical rules, but Hodson apparently assumed this to be due merely to a recent decay of traditional customs.

Mrs Seligman (in 1928) had not, it would seem, encountered Hodson's papers. Her approach to the topic of Kachin type marriage was somewhat indirect.

In 1927 there had been published a posthumous paper by Deacon (1927) which indicated that there existed on Ambryn an anomalous form of marriage with the sister of the sister's husband which resulted in the division of society into six 'marriage classes' or sections very much on the Australian pattern. Study of this system led Mrs Seligman to re-examine the scheme of Pentecost kinship terminology published by Rivers (1914), which she thought might fit the Ambryn pattern. Instead she reached the conclusion, on purely inductive grounds, that the marriage system on Pentecost must be of the Kachin type (matrilineal). Her explanation of this rule was both novel and curious.

Mrs Seligman proposed to distinguish three systems of descent, *unilateral, bilateral* and *asymmetrical*. Asymmetrical descent was deemed to be a system combining features of the other two.

'Descent may be said to be asymmetrical when one form works in a submerged manner while the dominant form only is responsible for clan organization (or any other form of grouping). In this form of descent the dominant form is recognized by both sexes, but . . . the submerged form is recognized by one sex only. Thus, with dominantly matrilineal descent, men and women both recognize matrilineal descent, but men also recognize patrilineal descent while women do not' (Seligman, 1928, p. 536).

A few pages later this situation is further explained by saying that in a matrilineal society 'a woman marries into the group of her father, a man into the group to which neither belongs'. These two statements do not

---

[1] The argument seems to be implicit in several papers by Hodson published from 1921 onwards. It is formulated clearly in Hodson (1925, pp. 173–4).

[2] The expressions 'dual' and 'tripartite' are those used by Bose (1934). Hutton in various contexts from 1921 onwards writes of Assam societies with 'dual' and 'triple' divisions but does not associate these with any particular form of cross-cousin marriage; cf. Hutton (1921a). Hodson himself seems usually to write of 'dual' and 'multiple' organization.

appear to be quite consistent but what seems to be intended is that, in terms of Fig. 9, Ego (male) has membership in B and C 'groups' simultaneously, while his sister Ego (female) is a member of B 'group' only.

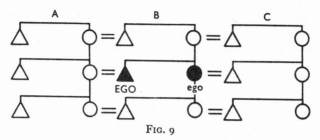

FIG. 9

In Mrs Seligman's own diagram (1928, p. 542) the system is represented as circular—males of 'group' A marry females of 'group' C—the exact nature of the 'groups' in question is obscure. She rather hesitatingly suggests that on Pentecost these 'groups' may be regarded as 'marriage classes' on the Australian pattern, and seems to argue similarly for Kachin type marriage systems in Assam. At the same time she recognizes, as Hodson had done, that while there must be at least three 'groups' in such a system, there may well be more than three (1928, pp. 550, 553).

Mrs Seligman seems to have evolved her principle of 'asymmetrical descent' as an inference from the study of kinship terminologies. She did not claim that any such system had been reported by anthropological fieldworkers. In point of fact however something of the sort had already been reported from China. Kulp (1925, p. 168) had explained a South China Kachin type marriage system as follows:

'The latter marriage (i.e., with the F.sis.d.) is taboo because of the traditional attitude that the boy has only his father's blood and the girl has only her mother's blood. . . . But the mother has the blood of her brother's son because the latter, being a son, has the blood of his father. . . . In other words a girl and her mother are conventionalized, so far as mating is concerned, into siblings, but they are not practical members of the paternal sib.'[1]

Kulp's wording is far from clear, but what he apparently intends to say is that a woman is identified with her mother and a man with his father, so that sex relations between a man and his father's sister's daughter are the equivalent of brother-sister incest. Mrs Seligman might, I think, justifiably have claimed this as a concrete example of asymmetrical descent.

Nevertheless even if an argument of this kind may sometimes help to explain the mental associations whereby marriage with the father's sister's

---

[1] Kulp's original text is slightly less ambiguous as it includes references to a diagram here omitted.

daughter may come to be thought of as incestuous, it tells us nothing about any positive structural implications of the Kachin type marriage rule. That being so, I do not feel myself that Mrs Seligman's paper contributed very much to the immediate topic of our present discussion, even though it may have been important as a contribution to the theories of incest and exogamy.

However that may be, the concept of asymmetrical descent, and the associated notion that the intermarrying 'groups' in a Kachin type system may be regarded as 'marriage classes', has undoubtedly had very considerable influence, both upon subsequent theory and upon subsequent fieldwork—not always with very fortunate results.[1]

THE MURNGIN CONTROVERSY

The first modern study of a Kachin type marriage system in actual operation was Warner's report (1930–31) on the Murngin,[2] published in 1930. Rival interpretations of the data were published by Elkin (1933) and Webb (1933) in 1933, and controversy has raged ever since. The latest contribution to this debate is a remarkable broadside by Radcliffe-Brown (1951), which, while effectively demolishing the earlier arguments of Murdock (Lawrence and Murdock, 1949), still leaves some matters unexplained.

I do not propose to recapitulate the whole of this argument, but will merely examine further certain aspects of the matter that have so far tended to be somewhat neglected.

The crux of the debate is this: Warner displays the Murngin kinship system by means of a diagram of 7 descent lines on the model of my Fig. 10. Radcliffe-Brown and his immediate pupils, e.g. Sharp (1934), Thomson (1949), take it for granted that the diagram implies no more than this. Other readers of Warner's paper, in particular Lawrence, Murdock and Lévi-Strauss, have however assumed that the 7 lines represent, not merely descent lines, but actual segments of the total society.

Radcliffe-Brown (1951) has recently ridiculed Murdock for this misunderstanding, but I think it is a moot point how far Warner himself was clear upon the matter at issue. Although in the first half of his paper Warner does, fairly consistently, refer to his diagram as if it were a system of descent lines only, in the second half he also asserts that

'all perpendicular relationships are strong and unbreakable since they are patrilineal lines of father, sons, daughters, brothers and sisters belonging to the same totemic clans and interlocking families'

and

---

[1] See p. 73.

[2] *Murngin* is a term applied by Warner to the population of eastern Arnhem Land. Though Warner speaks of the Murngin 'tribe' this is a misnomer. As Thomson points out 'tribal organization is conspicuous by its absence from the intricate social organization of the area' (Thomson, 1949, p. 11).

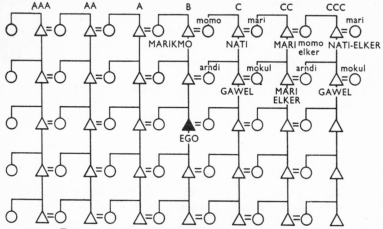

FIG. 10.—Diagram of same type as Fig. 7 giving skeleton
of Murngin descent line diagram.

'each of the seven lines of descent is built out of the restricted family, which preserves its continuity by the patrilineal laws that regulate descent among father and sons' (Warner, 1931, p. 172).

But, as we have seen in Part 1 of this essay, if the lines represent local descent groups, then group A and group C are not only distinct from Ego's own group they are also distinct from one another. It is, then, very understandable that readers of Warner's paper should have supposed that each of the seven lines in his diagram denoted a separate group or set of groups of actual people.

That granted, it was inevitable that Lawrence, Murdock and Lévi-Strauss should all infer that the whole system is really circular. Lawrence and Murdock (1949), in point of fact, not only assert that each of the seven lines of Warner's diagram represents a separate descent group, they claim that there is also an eighth such descent group which Warner failed to notice and that the whole eight groups 'marry in a circle' in the manner proposed by Hodson for the Kachins. Not only that, but each of these imaginary descent groups is further subdivided into 4 sections to produce in all 32 'classes'. Apparently the theory is that Ego can only marry into one of these classes, which seems to imply that he must marry the mother's brother's daughter who is also father's father's sister's daughter's daughter's husband's sister's husband's sister's husband's sister's husbands' sister—a proposition which Radcliffe-Brown (1951, p. 53) rightly regards as ludicrous!

Actually, if it were the case that the Murngin were divided into 8, 16 or 32 easily recognizable distinct local groups, even a fantastic system of this kind would deserve serious examination. But since this kind of ordering of local groups does not, so far as we know, exist, the Murdock version of the Murngin social structure need not be further considered.[1]

But while I concede that Radcliffe-Brown has successfully demolished the notion that the seven descent lines of Warner's diagram represent segments of the total Murngin society, he has so far failed to make clear just what is the degree of correspondence between these descent lines and the local descent groups which constitute actual Murngin society at any particular point in time.

This point can I think be cleared up by a little reasoning from first principles.

My Fig. 10 is a skeleton of Warner's full diagram of 7 descent lines. I have filled in only the kinship terms which denote relatives who are genealogically related to Ego *while he is still a youth*. The persons denoted by the lower and left hand portions of Warner's diagram only become socially important to Ego after he has married and acquired offspring.

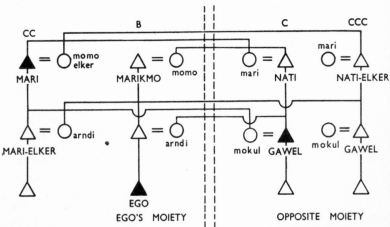

FIG. 11.—Top right hand corner of Fig. 10 rearranged. B, CC, C, and CCC are here four local descent groups, B and CC in one moiety, C and CCC in the other.

Fig. 11 represents this same top right hand corner of Fig. 10 redrawn to show the moiety arrangement. In this latter figure the lines B, C, CC and CCC need no longer be thought of simply as descent lines; they here denote local descent groups of real people alive at the same time and related to Ego during his childhood and youth. This diagram shows the logic of the kinship terminology much more clearly than any of the

[1] Considerable additional data is necessary before a fully satisfactory analysis of the Murngin situation can be made. It seems possible that the key to the situation may be found in the existence, in this area, of numerous 'linguistic groups' the distribution of which does not coincide with the distribution of population by locality (cf. Elkin and Berndt, 1950; Firth, 1951b).

constructions provided by Warner. Ego's own local group B is allied with that of Ego's mother's mother's brother (MARI), group CC, and balanced against a similar pair of linked local groups, that of the mother's brother (GAWEL) and that of the mother's mother's mother's brother's son (NATI-ELKER).[1]

The local descent group CC which is paired with Ego's own descent group B need not necessarily be a part of Ego's own patrilineal horde *but it may be*, and this is the crucial fact, clearly stated by Warner, which invalidates Murdock's interpretation of the facts. In Fig. 11 MARI (line CC) and MARIKMO (line B) cannot be one and the same person but they can be clan brothers.[2]

Crucial to Warner's original analysis is a discussion of the status relationships linking the three individuals Ego (line B), GAWEL (line C) and MARI (line CC).

The general principles of reciprocity formulated by Mauss in his *Essai sur le don* would lead us to expect that Kachin type marriage will normally be associated with some scheme of gift exchange between 'wife giving' and 'wife receiving' local descent groups such that, on balance, the 'wife giving' group will receive some compensation for the loss of the woman and her offspring. In every empirical case of Kachin type marriage for which the ethnographic data is at all adequate, this does appear to be the case; though, as we shall see, the form of compensation is not always quite what might be expected.

This immediately raises a problem of theoretical importance. If, in terms of Fig. 7 or Fig. 10, group A is, on balance, always giving gifts to group B and group B to group C, does not this suggest a permanent status difference in which C is senior to B and B senior to A? Furthermore if the overall system is *not* 'circular', what system of reciprocities permits the goods which C accumulates to return back to A again?

Warner examined this problem in the Murngin situation and his conclusions are on the whole convincing. On his analysis, persons in Ego's own group (Fig. 11, line B) are, on balance, constantly giving valuables to persons in GAWEL's group line C, and GAWEL does occupy a position of status superiority towards Ego. But in the same way persons in line C are giving valuables to persons in line CC, and MARI occupies a position

---

[1] To make clear the relationship between the different kinship terms I have altered Warner's spelling:

Warner	*Leach*
Natchiwalker	Nati-elker
Momelker	Momo-elker
Marelker	Mari-elker

This I think is legitimate in view of the comments and spelling of Radcliffe-Brown (1951, p. 49) and Thomson (1949, p. 77). Warner himself notes that these three terms were diminutives of Nati, Momo, and Mari respectively.

[2] Warner (1931, p. 180): 'they belong to the same moiety and frequently to the same clan'. Cf. Warner (1937, pp. 17, 28–29).

of status superiority towards GAWEL. But between Ego and MARI there is great solidarity, for Ego is a kind of ritual successor to MARI, inheriting his names (and possibly his valuables).

Warner's argument therefore seems to be that whether or not groups B and CC are actually segments of the same clan they are close allies and stand together in balanced opposition to the two groups C and CCC which are similarly allied and with which, taken as pairs, there is an exchange of women—though not an exclusive one. This is the position while Ego is still a youth. Later in life he becomes first a 'mother's brother' and then later a 'mother's brother's brother' and other systems of four local lines come into being—that is to say sectors of lines A, AA, and AAA in Fig. 10. In each case there will be this same balance of a pair of closely allied local descent groups which, taken as a pair, exchange wives with another similar pair on a non-exclusive basis.

In this manner although the status difference between 'wife givers' and 'wife receivers' is admitted, the overall system is represented as one of equilibrium.

There remain some gaps in Warner's argument and it would still appear that his explanation requires that the groups on the wife receiving side of Ego's system are constantly supplying him with valuables for which, ultimately, they have no source of supply. This slight paradox is however largely resolved by a recent contribution from Thomson (1949) who indicates that the exchanges between mother's brother and sister's son are but one element in a wide system of economic exchanges, and that the ultimate source of those valuables which are not easily manufactured on the spot is continuing foreign trade with Indonesians and Europeans.[1]

This discussion of the economic and status relations implicit in a Kachin type marriage system is, to my mind, the most important theme to be derived from Warner's study, but it is a theme which has in general been ignored in the later literature on the Murngin. Instead, the whole weight of the debate has centred on how far the eight sub-sections found in Murngin society can be regarded as marriage classes and 'sur la manière dont se ferme le cycle des mariages' (Lévi-Strauss, 1949, p. 245). The basic error in these 'Murdock style' arguments has already been explained.

Finally I would remark that, to my way of thinking, Radcliffe-Brown (1951, p. 55) is rather over-anxious to see the Murngin system as merely a variant of the general Australian pattern. Here I am in agreement with Lévi-Strauss who regards Kachin type marriage as a legitimate isolate. The fact that the Murngin system falls into the Kachin type category makes it comparable in important respects with Kachin type systems occurring outside the Australian field.

---

[1] Readers of Thomson's monograph may note that he translates *gurruto* as 'relatives' whereas Warner translates *gurratu* as 'kinship system'. This serves to confirm, I think, that Warner himself was confused as to how far his abstract kinship system denoted living persons.

LATER DISCUSSION OF OTHER VARIETIES OF
KACHIN TYPE MARRIAGE

Writers from other areas were equally slow to take up Warner's hint that Kachin type marriage is likely to imply a status superiority of the mother's brother's local descent group over that of Ego's own.

The topic of Kachin type marriage has been discussed on a number of occasions since 1930 by K. P. Chattopadhaya and other Indian anthropologists (Chattopadhaya, 1931; Das, 1935, 1945; Bose, 1934, 1935, 1937a, b; Roy, 1936). The arguments put forward by these writers all derive directly from Rivers, Hutton, Hodson and Mrs Seligman. Two themes constantly recur; the claim to demonstrate that Kachin type marriage is an outcome of the conquest by a patrilineal minority of a matrilineal society having dual organization, and an insistence upon the empirical existence of 'marriage classes' of the type postulated by Mrs Seligman. Both arguments are expounded with ingenuity and much learned algebra, but appear otherwise to lack merit. On the contrary, the assumption that the clans among the Old Kuki 'tribes' of Manipur are in some way a species of 'marriage class' has now so prejudiced the ethnographic description of this region that for comparative purposes the material is almost useless. For example systems of 'marriage in a circle' have been claimed for the Chiru, the Chawte, the Purum and the Tarau. In not a single case does the empirical evidence provided by the ethnographers tend to support this proposition (Das, 1934, 1945; Bose, 1934, 1935, 1937a, b; Roy, 1936). The only positive evidence that does emerge is that *in any one village* patrilineages stand in more or less stable 'wife giving'–'wife receiving' relationship, and that *in any one village* there are status differences between patrilineages. These however are not the inferences which the authors themselves draw from their data.

Similar arguments to the effect that Kachin type marriage is necessarily correlated with a system of threefold patrilineal marriage classes marrying in a circle, and that it represents an evolution from an earlier matrilineal dual organization have been propounded by Olderogge (1946) and Mrs Ruhemann (1948), but I do not find their arguments convincing. Van Wouden (1935) has formulated a theoretical scheme of 16 marriage classes marrying in a circle which he claims as the basis of modern East-Indonesian social systems. Josselin de Jong (1951) has recently attempted a rather similar analysis for Minangkabau. These schemes are purely hypothetical and do not correspond at all closely with any recorded ethnographic facts.[1]

Another version of the same theme is the monograph published by Granet (1939). This sets out to reconstruct the kinship organization of the ancient Chinese in both the archaic and early classical periods. The data used for this purpose are kinship terminologies, forms of ritual

[1] Another Dutch scholar who has written extensively on the Kachin type marriage systems of Indonesia is Fischer, but his writings have not, I think, advanced the theoretical position. Cf. Fischer (1935 and 1936). [But see p. 55.]

adopted from ancestor worship, quotations from the Chinese classics and so on. The conclusions are that the archaic system was of the Kariera type but based on matrilocal instead of patrilocal marriage—i.e. a matrilocal 4 section system—while at a later, early classical, period this organization was somehow converted into a system of 8 patrilineally defined 'categories' (in effect 'marriage classes') which married in a circle according to the Kachin type rule. In other words, the imaginary early classical Chinese system of Granet was a 'Murdock-Murngin' system. Granet's reconstruction is an impossibility for just the same reason as Murdock's interpretation of the Murngin system is an impossibility.

As Granet disdains to cite the work of other scholars and insists upon describing fairly simple anthropological situations by means of a highly complex diagrammatical notation of his own invention, it is difficult to trace precisely the source of his ideas. It seems reasonably clear however that he must have been familiar with the work of both Radcliffe-Brown and Warner. Lévi-Strauss's lavish praise of his originality thus seems unwarranted.

The chief merit of Granet's work is that he brings the discussion back to the point where Warner had left it. He stresses the theme that an arranged marriage is not a one sided transaction; it is part of an exchange. In Kariera type systems it is a direct exchange of women; in Kachin type systems it is an exchange of women for gifts (prestations), the gifts in turn being exchanged with another group for further women. Thus logically we should be led to consider Kachin type marriage not simply as a phenomenon of kinship in isolation, but as a phenomenon involving the inter-relation between kinship institutions and economic institutions. But Granet does not pursue this aspect of the matter.

Like Hodson, Granet found in the Kachin system, as described by the ethnographers, an ideal model for a system based on matrilateral cross-cousin marriage. Even so it is notable that he does not hesitate to adjust this ethnographic record wherever the reported facts fail to fit the requirements of his hypothetical historical reconstructions. The Kachin system as reported by Granet is much more remote from reality than the Kachin system as understood by Hodson.

Though Granet's monograph probably tells us little about ancient Chinese history, it had the useful effect of stimulating anthropologists to enquire into the facts concerning Kachin type marriage among modern Chinese.[1]

Though nowhere elevated to the status of an absolute rule, there does appear to be a very general tendency in certain areas of China to approve marriage with the mother's brother's daughter while banning marriage with the father's sister's daughter. Fei (1939) and Hsu (1945) have both looked for 'functional' explanations of a simple causal type. [But see pp. 54–5.]

Fei's explanation is that marriage with the F.sis.d. is barred because,

[1] Hsu (1940) in a critical review of Granet's book.

in such a system, Ego (male)'s grandmother (F.m.), who is the tyrant of Ego's own household, would then be of the same lineage as Ego's bride (F.sis.d.). Ego's mother has suffered from the tyranny of the grandmother, and would tend to persecute the young bride in revenge. m.B.d. marriage has the reverse effect; mother-in-law and daughter-in-law are of the same lineage. The ban on marriage with the F.sis.d. is thus said to promote harmony between mother-in-law and daughter-in-law (see Figs. 12a and 12b).

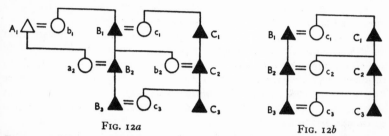

FIG. 12a

FIG. 12b

FIG. 12a.—With Trobriand type (patrilineal) marriage c_1 is originally from same local descent group as c_3. a_2 who has suffered persecution at hands of c_1 will revenge herself on c_3.

FIG. 12b.—With Kachin type (patrilineal) marriage, c_1, c_2 and c_3 are all of same lineage and should (in theory) be friendly to one another.

Hsu has rightly argued that explanation of this kind involve a large number of unstated and unverifiable psychological assumptions. In an effort to show that no one functional explanation can have any general validity he cites five different explanations which were given to him at various times by 'sophisticated young scholars, and old fashioned school teachers, elderly ladies with fixed views and younger ladies of modern attitude and extraction, middle aged labourers and their peasant wives'. These several alleged 'functions' of Kachin type marriage are of considerable interest. I quote:

'1. Marriage for a woman means transference from a family of lower standing to a family of higher standing. For it is the custom that parents prefer their daughters-in-law to come from lower families while they wish their daughters to marry into higher families than themselves. m.B.S. marriage means for a girl to enter in a lower family than the one of her origin. . . .

2. Marriage of the F.sis.d. type will shrink the circle of kinship and reduce the number of relatives who may be of help. . . .

3. In all Chinese provinces the custom is for a married daughter to return to her parents' family from time to time for periods of sojourn. She enjoys a definite privileged place in this house as contrasted with her place in her husband's house where she is the least privileged of all members. Now F.sis.d. and m.B.S. marriage will place a mother's and daughter's position in jeopardy; in one household the mother is privileged and not the

daughter; while in another the position is reversed. It makes psychological adjustment between the two difficult. . . .

4. F.sis.d. and m.B.S. type of marriage is actually a return of bone and flesh. . . .

Children and parents as well as brothers and sisters are bone and flesh to each other. The father's sister by giving her own daughter in marriage to her brother's son will have effected what virtually is her own permanent return to her parents' home . . . it is an ominous forecast of divorce. . . .

5. The Kiangsu type of argument that F.sis.S. and m.B.d. marriage makes for harmonious family relationship and F.S.d.—m.B.S. marriage destroys such harmony—which Fei endorsed. . . .'[1]

What seems to me very interesting about this list is that the first three explanations are all essentially structural explanations, in that they are expressed in terms of persisting relations between local descent groups; while the last two explanations, which oddly enough are the only ones which seem to have received support from the anthropologists, are essentially psychological explanations, in that they relate to temporary relationships between individuals.

It is only the structural type of explanation that has any real relevance to our present discussion. Of the latter, explanations 1 and 3 are structurally the same—they both derive from the assumption that the 'wife receiving group' will be of higher status than the 'wife giving group'. A rephrasing of explanations 2 and 3 might read 'every local descent group must have 'wife receiving partners' and 'wife giving partners' and these two categories must not be confused'.

From this the following simple inference seems permissible: *Chinese who practise Kachin type marriage take it for granted that in terms of Fig. 7 seniority runs from left to right. Group AA ranks higher than A, A higher than B, B higher than C, C higher than CC.*

It will be noted that this is the reverse direction of seniority from that previously inferred for the Murngin. With the Murngin the mother's brother (group C) ranks higher than Ego (group B) and on balance receives gifts from him.

It is then highly significant that in the Chinese system the balance of payments goes from wife givers to wife receivers and that the express function of this dowry is to raise the status of the bride in her new home (Fei, 1939, pp. 43–44).[2]

LÉVI-STRAUSS'S THEORY

In 1949 Lévi-Strauss published his formidable and ambitious work *Les Structures élémentaires de la parenté*. This is at once a contribution to incest theory, a study of the relevance of reciprocity to all institutionalized

---

[1] Hsu (1945). It will be seen that 4 is essentially the same argument as that given by Kulp (1925); see *supra*, p. 67.

[2] Ideally the dowry is supposed to be double the brideprice.

forms of marriage, an analysis of the structural implications of the several varieties of cross-cousin marriage, and a general theory of social evolution. The scope of the work thus includes the topic of this essay, but it also embraces a much vaster field.

My principal criticism of the book is that it attempts far too much. Instead of being content to try to establish correlations between particular kinship structures and a limited variety of institutional dimensions, the author seems to aim at establishing, or at least indicating, the general laws of development governing all Asiatic societies, ancient and modern, primitive and sophisticated. This enormous programme is only covered by adopting a decidedly cavalier attitude towards the facts of history and ethnography. In the course of a long, though rapid, journey through the ethnography of all Australia and most of mainland Asia Lévi-Strauss scatters in profusion analytical suggestions of the greatest brilliance. But too often these ideas are misapplied, either because of weakness of ethnographic detail, or because the author is in too much of a hurry to get on to bigger and more exciting things. I am concerned here only with that part of Lévi-Strauss's argument which deals with Kachin type marriage. Lévi-Strauss himself seems to consider his inferences on this theme as strictly logical deductions from the work of Hodson, Warner and Granet, aided by his own re-examination of the original Kachin sources. But are these logical deductions in fact valid?

Lévi-Strauss's reading of the Murngin situation appears to resemble closely that of Murdock, and must be dismissed for the reasons already given. He notes Warner's views about the superior status of Murngin mother's brother to sister's son and the balancing of the relationship by the solidarity between mother's mother's brother and sister's daughter's son, but dismisses the argument as a psychological interpretation of social facts.[1] I conclude from this that either I or Lévi-Strauss has misunderstood what Warner was trying to say. If my précis of Warner's argument (see above, p. 69f.) is a valid one, then it is strictly a structural and not a psychological argument and indeed it is an argument of just the same kind as those which Lévi-Strauss himself puts forward in other parts of his book. The confusion I think has arisen in part from Warner's unclear statements, and in part from Lévi-Strauss's own tendency to confuse descent lines with local lines.

For his Kachin arguments, Lévi-Strauss, having noted the contributions of Hodson and Granet, goes back to original sources. In this field I can claim special knowledge, having myself carried out fieldwork in the Kachin area at various times between 1939 and 1943. Having this special knowledge, I am bound to state that Lévi-Strauss has often seriously misunderstood his sources and that in important particulars this misunderstanding is due to quite inexcusable carelessness. Nevertheless, despite these errors of ethnographic fact it appears to me that he has put

[1] Lévi-Strauss (1949), p. 236.

forward several wholly original theoretical suggestions which are not only empirically valid, but are of the utmost importance for a proper understanding of the Kachin situation.

First let me make good my accusation of inexcusable carelessness. In his very extensive references to the Kachins Lévi-Strauss relies, in the main, upon standard sources (Wehrli, 1904; Gilhodes, 1922; Hanson, 1913; Carrapiett, 1929), but he also refers at a number of crucial points to a work by Head entitled *Handbook of the Haka Chin Customs* (1917). From the context in which he uses this source there can be no doubt at all that he has assumed that Head's statements about the Haka Chins are applicable to the Kachins.[1] There can be no excuse for this blunder. Not only are the Chins geographically remote from the Kachins, they do not so far as we know even practise Kachin type marriage.[2]

As Lévi-Strauss (1949, p. 322) himself argues, the crux of his whole Kachin analysis turns upon two apparent paradoxes:

'Nous sommes donc en présence de deux oppositions: l'une entre la simplicité des règles de l'union préférentielle et la complexité du système des prestations; l'autre entre la pauvreté des termes de références et la richesse des termes d'appellation.'

But the complex system of prestations which he cites is Chin not Kachin, and the supposed poverty of terms of reference and richness of terms of address is simply an error of the literature.[3]

In matters of Kachin ethnography Lévi-Strauss must then be deemed wholly unreliable. In what follows I will therefore confine my attention to his theoretical propositions.

Shorn of its ethnographic background Lévi-Strauss's thesis seems to run something like this:

(*a*) In the tradition of Tylor the exogamy of the individual family is seen as an expression of the positive social necessity to 'marry out', rather than as a reflection of negative incest prohibitions.

(*b*) A marriage considered by itself is a relation between individuals. But sociologically a marriage does not exist in isolation but as part of a series of marriages past and future. From this point of view a marriage is but one incident in a series of reciprocal transactions between groups.

(*c*) We can distinguish two general modes in which reciprocal relations between groups are expressed. Firstly in the transfer of goods; secondly in the transfer of women.

---

[1] Cf. Lévi-Strauss (1949), pp. 297, 322ff., 377, etc.

[2] The Haka Chins are neighbours to the Lakher on one side, who do practise Kachin type marriage, and to the Zahau Chins on the other, who do not. Concerning the Haka themselves there is no evidence.

[3] Cf. Leach (1945). There are 18 terms of reference not 14, as Lévi-Strauss supposed. The 'termes d'appellation' referred to are in fact proper names. Far from being numerous there are only 9 for each sex, a fact which results in a proliferation of 'nicknames'.

(d) Hence in logic we need to consider three types of exchange relationship:

(i) Relationship between social groups is expressed by the simultaneous or nearly simultaneous exchange of goods—the Trobriand Kula might be taken as an example.

(ii) Relationship between social groups is expressed by the simultaneous or nearly simultaneous exchange of women—the Australian Kariera and Aranda marriage systems might be taken as examples (échange restreint in Lévi-Strauss's terminology).

(iii) Relationship between social groups is expressed by the exchange of women for goods—formalized systems of asymmetrical cross-cousin marriage (échange généralisé in Lévi-Strauss's terminology) provide examples of this pattern.

(e) Seen from this point of view the two varieties of asymmetrical cross-cousin marriage have quite different implications:

Kachin type marriage has the effect that as between two groups A and B, A will continuously give goods to B while B will continuously give women to A.

Trobriand type marriage has the effect that A gives women to B in one generation, but B gives women back to A in the following generation (Lévi-Strauss, 1949, ch. 27).

(f) It appears to be Lévi-Strauss's (1949, p. 554) view that Trobriand type marriage is, relatively speaking, sociologically unimportant since it does not result in long term structural continuities. Two marriages in successive generations merely constitute a reciprocal exchange between two biological families. With the fulfilment of the second marriage the whole transaction is complete.

In Kachin type marriage on the other hand the unilaterally defined descent groups A and B stand in a permanent persisting relationship of 'wife giving group' and 'wife receiving group'. The whole structure of society is built upon the assumption of this continuity.

(g) We have seen that most of Lévi-Strauss's predecessors in this field have assumed that Kachin type marriage necessarily implies a circular system of marriage classes of the general type A marries B, B marries C, C marries A. To a considerable and often confusing extent Lévi-Strauss accepts this position; yet there are moments when he sees beyond it. For suppose the circle is not closed, what then? With the wealth objects involved in marriage transactions always moving in the same direction, does not this imply an ultimate difference in economic status between the wealth giving and wealth receiving groups?

(h) Following this line of reasoning, Lévi-Strauss reaches, on purely theoretical grounds, the following interesting conclusion:

Ideally Kachin type marriage ought always to operate in a circle. Provided it does so, wealth objects will simply circulate in one direction while women will circulate in the other, the status of the component local descent groups will remain equal.

In practice such a system may well be workable provided there are, say, only three groups in the circle. But in theory the system might be extended indefinitely in either direction (as in Fig. 7 or 10). The more local groups there are the more impracticable it will be to keep all transactions within the circle.

In practice, argues Lévi-Strauss (1949, p. 325), there will be competition for women; this will lead to an accumulation of women in one part of the circuit rather than in another, with a consequent development of brideprice differentials:

'on arrive donc à la conclusion que l'échange généralisé conduit, de façon presque inéluctable, à l'hypergamie, c'est-à-dire au mariage entre conjoints de status différents.'

Having made this theoretical suggestion he attempts to validate it in terms of the Kachin material which he has previously discussed. He notes that despite their form of marriage the Kachins are nevertheless reported as being a class stratified society. He notes also that there are proverbs which approve and others which disapprove of polygyny. He seems to argue that despite the social difficulties that ensue the acquisition of several women must be highly valued in Kachin society. The reader is clearly intended to infer that throughout the social structure the wife receiving group will rank higher than the wife giving group, the nobles at the top being the accumulators of women.[1] Hence if we take the lines of Fig. 7 to represent 5 intermarrying 'groups' AA, A, B, C, CC, these groups can be thought of as 'exogamous castes' which practise hypergamous marriage, AA being the most senior.

Later in the book (1949, pp. 518ff.) he argues that the five major clans (*grands groupes fondamentaux*) into which Kachin society is supposed to be divided can be identified as these exogamous castes. And he goes on to argue that a similar Kachin type marriage rule may have been a factor in creating the Indian caste system as we now know it.

With such extreme speculations I am no more concerned than with those of Granet, which are indeed of much the same kind, but it is worth discussing in some detail how far Lévi-Strauss's initial hypothesis does in fact tally with the Kachin situation.

---

[1] Lévi-Strauss (1949) does not appear to state specifically whether he supposes the 'wife receivers' to rank above the 'wife givers' or vice versa; but since he draws close analogies between the Kachin system and that of the Chinese and also with Indian caste hypergamy, the former alternative seems to be assumed (p. 587). He notes with surprise that Parry reports Lahker hypergamy to operate in the reverse direction (p. 336), but makes no inference from this.

In actual fact, among the Kachins, as among the Lahkers, 'wife givers' rank higher than 'wife receivers'.

To support his view that Kachins at times set a high value on polygyny Lévi-Strauss (p. 326) cites the proverb:

du num shi; tarat num mali

chief woman ten; commoner woman four.

This he interprets as 'a chief may have ten wives, a commoner four'. In fact the real meaning of the proverb is 'the price of a chief's wife is ten cattle; the price of a commoner's wife four cattle'.

PART 3

A New Analysis of Three Kachin Type Marriage Systems

THE GENUINE KACHIN SYSTEM

Kachin[1] society as described in the standard ethnographic accounts and by Lévi-Strauss is made up of 5 exogamous particlans which marry in a circle in the manner already discussed. In a paper published in 1950 (Leach, 1945) I showed that this circular marriage system does not represent empirical fact but is simply a kind of verbal model which the Kachins themselves use to explain the general pattern of their system. The empirical situation is as follows.

Kachins clearly think of their society as a widely ramifying dispersed clan system. The major clans are segmented into dispersed lineages, and these segmented into further dispersed sub-lineages and so on. On first enquiry one gets the impression that clan exogamy is intended to prevail throughout, but in practice this is simply 'a manner of speaking'. The exogamous unit is really the lineage at the lowest level of segmentation. In essentials this smallest lineage is a local descent group associated with a particular political domain (*mung*), though some members of it may reside elsewhere.

Kachins habitually speak as if the 'wife giving'–'wife receiving' (*mayu-dama*) relationship that results from marriage was the concern of major lineages or even clans. But in practice marriage is the affair of local descent groups only. If there happen to be two groups in the same domain which, from the lineage point of view, are segments of the same clan, it is more than likely that they will intermarry and be in *mayu-dama* relationship. In the account which follows my use of the terms 'lineage' and 'local descent group' is intended to conform to this distinction between Kachin ideology and Kachin practice.

In Kachin ideology if a man of patrilineage A marries a woman of patrilineage B, it is proper and expected that at a later date there will be a further marriage between another man of lineage A and another woman of lineage B. Furthermore a marriage between a man of lineage B and a woman of lineage A would be a breach of customary law.

The relationship between the two lineages A and B is thus specific and has structural continuity. With respect to persons of lineage A lineage B is *mayu*; with respect to persons of lineage B, lineage A is *dama*. At

---

[1] The term Kachin applies to a population of about 300,000 scattered over a vast area (some 55,000 square miles) in the Assam–Burma–Yunnan frontier areas. The same network of kinship relations operates over the whole of this territory but the population is not tightly unified politically or culturally. There are however no clearly distinguishable tribal subdivisions of the population. [For details see Leach (1954).]

every marriage the *dama* purchase from *mayu* the potential offspring of the bride.

A male Ego is related to the fellows of his community in three principal ways. Persons of his own local descent group and of other lineages of his own clan are 'brothers' (*hpu-nau*); persons of local descent groups into which he and his male siblings are expected to marry are *mayu*; persons of local descent groups into which his female siblings are expected to marry are *dama*. Most close acquaintances fall into one of these three categories, those who do not do so by strict cognate or affinal relationship are treated much as if they were remote relatives of Ego's own clan. Thus the *mayu* of the *mayu* are classed as 'grandparents'; the *dama* of the *mayu* are classed as 'brothers'; the *dama* of the *dama* are classed as 'grandchildren'. In terms of our diagram Fig. 7 the order of seniority thus runs from left to right, group AA are 'grandchildren', A are *dama*, B are 'brothers', C are *mayu*, CC are 'grandparents'.[1] This suggests that if there is a difference of status between wife giving (*mayu*) and wife taking (*dama*) groups, it is the former and not the latter who are of higher rank. This is in fact the case.

The Kachin ideal is that a series of *mayu-dama* lineages should marry in a circle; the explanatory myth specifies five major lineages (clans), but any number greater than two will serve. Circular systems embracing three and occasionally four local descent groups are not uncommon, but, as Lévi-Strauss perceived, the system becomes increasingly unstable as the number of units in a single network of relationship is increased. Lévi-Strauss suggested that the instability will arise from competition to accumulate women for polygynous marriages; the empirical situation is that instability arises from competition for bridewealth.

The empirical Kachin local community has a fairly standardized structural form though its dimensions in terms of geographical area, population and component segments are very variable. The political unit is a single contiguous area ruled over by a chief.[2] This area I shall call the domain (*mung*) of a particular lineage of chiefly rank. The office of chief (*duwa*) will always be held by a member of this lineage, and the title will normally pass from youngest son to youngest son in the male line. The nature of the rights pertaining to this office of chief will be considered presently.

The population of the domain will normally comprise members of many different lineages, some of high rank and some of low rank, but within that domain no other local descent group can rank as high as that of the chief. All the local descent groups within a domain tend to be related to one another in a quite definite manner, explained below. This

---

[1] It should perhaps be stressed that Ego is permitted to marry these classificatory 'grandparents' and 'grandchildren'.

[2] What follows applies primarily to the Kachin *gumsa* type of political organization. In an alternative type of system known as *gumlao* the structure is somewhat different.

pattern is little affected by the ramifications of the lineage system outside the local area.

Territorially the area of a domain is commonly segmented into several sections which I have elsewhere called village clusters (*mare*); the village clusters in turn are segmented into villages (*kahtawng*). Structurally these segments are homologous. The relationship between a village and its parent village cluster is in almost all respects identical with that between a village cluster and its parent domain. Thus, although some political units comprise only a single village, while others include several villages forming a village cluster, and others again embrace several village clusters, the principles of organization in each of these political systems is the same.

To illustrate these principles let us consider a hypothetical domain which consists of a single village cluster comprising four villages. Each of the four villages has an hereditary headman (*salang wa*) whose office is inherited in the same way as that of the chief. One of the four headmen is also chief of the whole domain. The lineage of the chief 'owns' the whole territory of the domain. The local descent group of a village headman 'owns' the territory of his village but these two types of ownership are of a different order. The chief's ownership is recognized by the fact that all persons in the domain, who are not of his own lineage, must present him with a hind leg of any animal killed in sacrifice or in the hunt and by recognition that the same persons are under obligation to provide free labour for the chief on certain stated occasions, as at the clearing of the chief's field or the building of the chief's house. The village headman's ownership on the other hand is recognized in the fact that he disposes of the cultivation rights in the village lands among the householders of his village. Neither type of ownership can properly be said to include the right of alienation, though lands can be transferred from one chief to another or from one village to another in certain special circumstances.

The political relationship between chief and village headman—and for that matter between village headman and villager—has considerable resemblances to that of English feudal tenure. If the chief be regarded as Lord of the Manor, then the status of the village headman resembles something between the status of a freeholder, holding his land in fee tail, and the status of a tenant in villeinage holding his land in customary freehold or copyhold. If we accept this analogy, then we might expect to find some clear difference of class status as between chief's local descent groups, village headmen's local descent groups, and commoners' local descent groups. This difference of class status exists, though it is important to emphasize that the class distinctions are defined mainly in terms of rights to non-utilitarian prestige symbols,[1] and the difference in the economic standards of aristocrats and commoners is normally very slight.

[1] E.g., the right to make a particular kind of sacrifice or to put up a particular kind of housepost.

If we neglect the complicated subject of slavery,[1] there are three ordinarily recognized classes in Kachin society, which we can call chiefly class, aristocratic class and commoner class. The quality of class is theoretically an attribute of a lineage rather than of a person. Thus lineages are described as being *du baw amyu*—'chiefly lineages', *ma gam amyu*—'eldest son lineages', and *darat amyu*—'commoner lineages'. Since the commoners greatly outnumber the aristocrats and the aristocrats greatly outnumber the chiefs there is necessarily a procedure whereby the upper classes shed their surplus into the class below. This procedure depends upon the well understood principle of lineage fission. When a lineage has acquired a 'depth' of four or five generations it tends to split, but of the two residual lineages only one retains the class status of the parent lineage; the other tends to 'go down hill' (*gumyu yu ai*). In theory, the senior lineage is always the youngest son line—i.e. the youngest son of the youngest son, etc.—hence lineages which have split away from chiefly lineages and thereby assumed a subordinate status are eldest son lineages[2] —i.e. aristocrats. Similarly the lineages which split away from aristocratic lineages tend to 'go down hill' and become commoner lineages.

Matrilateral cross-cousin marriage plays an integral part not only in maintaining this class structure but in defining the 'feudal' relationships between chiefs, headmen, and commoners.

The two most general principles that govern the Kachin marriage system are that a man will do everything possible to avoid marrying into a class beneath him, and that a man will seek to make the maximum profit—either in terms of brideprice or political advantage—out of the marriage of his daughters. Lévi-Strauss's view that polygyny is highly esteemed for its own sake is erroneous. The factors which influence chiefs (and sometimes village headmen) to acquire more than one wife are firstly the importance of having a male heir to carry on the local descent group, and secondly the political advantage that comes from maintaining relations with several different *mayu* (wife giving) groups at the same time.

A chief, in order to maintain status, must marry—as his first wife—a woman from another chiefly lineage, that is to say a woman from some other chiefly domain. Such marriages can form the basis of large-scale

---

[1] Kachin 'slavery' was officially abolished by British administrative action. Formerly there were several categories of 'slaves' (*mayam*), but the majority were voluntary serfs—or even adopted sons—of their masters rather than chattels. Similar systems of so-called 'slavery' have often been reported from this region (cf. Parry, 1932, p. 223; Hutton, 1921b, pp. 145ff., 385ff.). In the Kachin marriage hierarchy the 'slaves' nominally formed two additional classes junior to the commoners. [See also Leach (1954), Appendix III.]

[2] In Kachin theory the status of a lineage is defined absolutely by genealogy so that a lineage can only lose status and never gain it. The practical situation is much more flexible than this but discussion of this theme must be postponed to a later publication. [See Leach (1954), pp. 162f.; (1960).]

political alliances. It is not uncommon to find three neighbouring chiefly groups A, B, and C, linked by the rule that chief A marries princess B, chief B marries princess C, chief C marries princess A. Such a system is called by the Kachins 'cousin circle path' (*hkau wang hku*). The three chiefs are all of equal status. Women go round the circle in one direction; bridewealth in the other. Incidentally, since the marriage transactions are in a sense somewhat nominal, the prestige of all concerned can be enhanced by specifying brideprices of huge (and quite imaginary) dimensions.

There are thus always some women of a chief's local descent group who marry away from the domain into other chiefly lineages; others however will marry with men of the aristocrat lineages of the chief's own domain. Typically the local descent group of a village headman is of the aristocrat class and will be *dama* (wife taking) in respect to the chief's local descent group.

Similar alternatives operate at the aristocratic level. The typical aristocratic lineage is the lineage of a village headman. Some aristocratic males will marry women of the chief's local descent group; some will marry women of other aristocratic local descent groups in the vicinity—especially those of other village headmen in the domain. Some aristocratic females marry aristocratic males, others marry commoners of their own village. At each level a limited though not exclusive circular system of the *hkau wang hku* tends to establish itself. The principle can be illustrated by resort to a diagram (Fig. 13) representing an imaginary political federation comprising three chiefs one of whom has under him three headmen, one of whom has under him three commoner local descent groups.

The structure it may be noted is not, as Lévi-Strauss supposed, analogous to hypergamy in the Indian caste system, but hypergamy reversed. Women may marry into their own class or the class below, but never into the class above.[1]

---

[1] Chiefs and headmen may take women from a lower class as secondary wives to raise an heir but the offspring of such women do not have the full class status of the male parent; the practical flexibility as opposed to the theoretical rigidity of the Kachin system depends upon this point (p. 84, n. 1).

I presume that all readers will appreciate that this explanation of the significance of matrilateral cross-cousin marriage for the hierarchy of authority in the Kachin *gumsa* type of political organization is based on a necessarily very simplified 'model' of any empirical reality. But the 'model' is one which, in effect, the Kachins have constructed themselves. *Gumsa* Kachins do appear to organize their lives on the theory that lineages are hierarchically ordered in the manner I have described. They insist most vigorously that commoners' lineages can never gain status and become aristocratic lineages, even though empirically this is clearly not the case. Objectively the situation seems to be that in *gumsa* Kachin society *all* the lineages present in any local community have a ranking status—i.e., of any two lineages, one ranks higher than the other; this is true even if both the lineages concerned are generally rated as commoner lineages. But this rank order is not stable. Every head of a household is constantly seeking to gain status for himself and for his lineage. There is a variety of recognized techniques of achieving merit in this way —a man may for example give a 'wealth feast' (*sut manau*), but the most effective

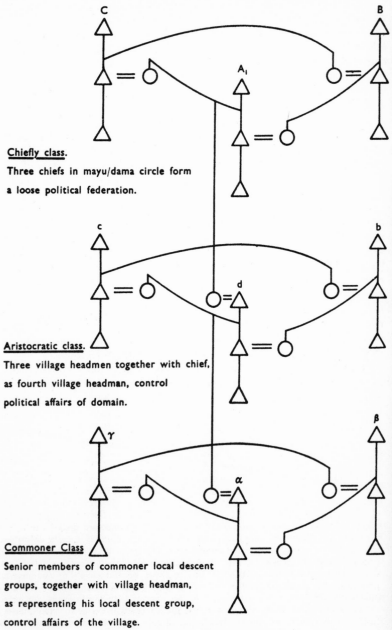

Chiefly class.
Three chiefs in mayu/dama circle form
a loose political federation.

Aristocratic class.
Three village headmen together with chief,
as fourth village headman, control
political affairs of domain.

Commoner Class
Senior members of commoner local descent
groups, together with village headman,
as representing his local descent group,
control affairs of the village.

FIG. 13.—Kachin political structure.

The class stratification and the formalized marriage links between classes ties in with the land tenure organization in the following manner. Ideally the pattern of Kachin residence is patrilocal; Kachins often talk as if a son, on growing up, automatically settled down in the village of his parents. With commoners who have no prestige to maintain, practice conforms fairly well with theory, but persons of rank are at least as likely to settle matrilocally as patrilocally. One major factor here is that the high ranking status of the youngest brother does not favour amicable relations between adult male siblings in chiefly families.

But if a chief's son settles in the alien village of his father-in-law, he places himself in an inferior position and admits his inferiority. Probably he will get his wife for a much reduced brideprice, but this in itself is a disgrace. In effect a man who settles matrilocally becomes the follower and tenant of his father-in-law. Yet in settling matrilocally in this way a man founds a new patrilineal local descent group. If the *mayu-dama* relationship thus initiated continues for several generations with orthodox patrilocal residence, the ultimate position will be that the descendants of the father-in-law and the descendants of the son-in-law will be living side by side in the same community in landlord-tenant relationship. This probably is the most usual history of present day Kachin villages.

and permanent procedure for social climbing is that of arranging an advantageous marriage for one's son. [This statement has been the source of some misunderstanding. For elaboration see Leach (1960).]

By way of further clarification I must also stress again the point emphasized in my earlier paper (Leach, 1945). The preferred Kachin marriage is not between mother's brother's daughter and father's sister's son but between *classificatory* mother's brother's daughter and *classificatory* father's sister's son (Kachin *nam* and Kachin *gu*). It is only among the chiefs, whose circle of kinsfolk is necessarily somewhat restricted, that an orthodox marriage with *nam* implies marriages with a 'real' mother's brother's daughter or any near relative. A commoner male normally has a wide range of *nam* to choose from, including for example any lineage sister of the wife of any of his father's lineage brothers. In many cases the actual relationship between *gu* and *nam* is very remote, but in Kachin eyes *any gu-nam* marriage is strictly orthodox. An important corollary of this is that the class status implications of the Kachin marriage rule operate with much more marked effect among the aristocratic classes (who tend on the whole to marry near relatives) than among the commoner classes (who do not).

Lines A, B, C are the local descent groups of three ruling chiefs, who 'own' three separate political domains. A is *dama* to B; B is *dama* to C; C is *dama* to A.

Domain A comprises 4 villages represented by lines A, b, c, d. The chief of the domain A_1 is simultaneously headman of his own village.

The three subordinate headmen marry in a circle. d is *dama* to b; b is *dama* to c; c is *dama* to d. In addition at least one of these headmen, namely d, is *dama* to the chief A.

In the same way the village of headman d comprises four local descent groups. Three of these, *a*, *β*, *γ*, are of commoner class; the fourth d is the headman's own and is of aristocratic class. *a*, *β*, *γ* marry in a circle and at least one of them (*a*) is *dama* to the headman's group d.

There are also other ways in which a *mayu-dama* status between two local descent groups can come to reflect a landlord-tenant relationship in a feudal sense.

Blood feuds for example normally start over women. Typically a feud is between *mayu* and *dama*. The appropriate ending of a feud is a marriage —the *mayu-dama* relationship is resumed. This has sometimes meant that the defeated group settle in the territory of the victors as their *dama* tenants.[1]

When a chief goes to war he has the institutionalized right to call his *dama* to his aid. The promised reward of victory may be village territory. Once again the final outcome is that the superior chief and his tenants are in *mayu-dama* relationship.

Finally in areas where population is sparse a chief who has much territory but few followers may explicitly ask the followers of another chief to come and join him and will seal the compact with the gift of a daughter.[2]

Generalizing, it is fair to say that where the 'tenants' or followers of a village headman or domain chief are not regarded as clan brothers of the 'landlord', they are in the status of 'son-in-law' (*dama*) to the 'landlord'. The procedure for acquiring land rights of any kind is in almost all cases tantamount to marrying a woman from the lineage of the lord. In Kachin terms, the rights that any tenant has in his land are expressed in the fact that he is *dama* to his immediate superior in the 'feudal' hierarchy.

This analysis resolves what appeared to Lévi-Strauss as an outstanding paradox. As Lévi-Strauss understood the position the Kachin system is ideally one of 5 intermarrying marriage classes and thus essentially egalitarian. Since a man's prospective bride appears to be specified in advance by the rules of the *mayu-dama* system, it is surely paradoxical that brideprice payment should be large and complex?[3] Lévi-Strauss's (1949, p. 327) explanation seems to be that these large brideprice payments are a kind of pathological symptom representing the 'conflit entre les conditions égalitaires de l'échange généralizé, et ses conséquences aristocratiques'. He perceives that a marriage class system of the formal complexity which he attributes to the Kachin system is unworkable. He infers that the marriage classes will convert themselves into privileged classes but he considers that this is 'en contradiction avec le système, et doit donc entrainer sa ruine' (p. 325).

Yet the system as I have now described it is neither contradictory nor self-destructive. It is true that, on balance, bridewealth moves always in the same direction from commoners towards aristocrats, from aristocrats towards chiefs. And it is thus true that if bridewealth were composed wholly of irreplaceable commodities of the Trobriand *vaygu'a* type, the

---

[1] Cf. the Lakher example cited by Parry (1932, p. 219).
[2] Cf. Kawlu Ma Mawng (1942, pp. 55, 58).
[3] Although Lévi-Strauss confused Kachin practice with Chin, he might still I think argue that the scale of Kachin brideprice payments is paradoxically large.

system could be self-destructive, since in time the total sum of 'bride-wealth currency' would come into the hands of the aristocrats. But in fact the main item in a brideprice, or in any of the other complex legal obligations to which Lévi-Strauss (1949, p. 326) refers (*des prestations et des échanges, des 'dettes', des créances et des obligations*), is a gift of cattle; and cattle, among the Kachin, are a consumable commodity. On balance the chief does tend to accumulate wealth in the form of cattle. But prestige does not come from the owning of cattle; it derives from the slaughter of animals in religious feasts (*manau*). If a chief becomes rich as a consequence of marriages or other legal transactions he merely holds *manau* at more frequent intervals and on a larger scale, and his followers, who partake of the feast, benefit accordingly. Here then is the element which is necessary to complete the cycle of exchange transactions, the absence of which struck Lévi-Strauss as paradoxical.

Let me recapitulate my analysis:

(1) From a *political* aspect, chief is to headman as feudal Lord of the Manor is to customary freeholder.

(2) From a *kinship* aspect, chief is to headman as *mayu* to *dama*, that is as father-in-law to son-in-law.

(3) From a *territorial* aspect, the kinship status of the headman's lineage in respect to that of the chief is held to validate the tenure of land.

(4) From an *economic* aspect the effect of matrilateral cross-cousin marriage is that, on balance, the headman's lineage constantly pays wealth to the chief's lineage in the form of bridewealth. The payment can also, from the analytical point of view, be regarded as a rent paid to the senior landlord by the tenant. The most important part of this payment is in the form of consumer goods—namely cattle. The chief converts this perishable wealth into imperishable prestige through the medium of spectacular feasting. The ultimate consumers of the goods are in this way the original producers, namely, the commoners who attend the feast.

Structurally speaking therefore despite the seeming asymmetry of the kinship system the whole organization is in political and economic balance.

It will I hope be agreed that the analysis I have given is decidedly more satisfactory than that provided by Lévi-Strauss. It is worth pointing out wherein this superiority lies.

The original theorizing of Hodson and Mrs Seligman was defective not merely because of the inadequacy of their empirical data but because they considered kinship simply as a system in itself. If a kinship scheme be considered without reference to its political, demographic or economic implications it is inevitably thought of as a logically closed system. If it is not closed, it cannot work. Hence the eagerness with which these early writers accepted any ethnographic evidence which seemed to suggest an arrangement of mechanically articulated marriage classes.

Lévi-Strauss following the lead given by Warner and Granet makes a great advance upon these 'pure kinship' theories because he takes into account the reciprocity aspects of kinship. He is not content to see Kachin type marriage simply as a variant from the 'classic' systems of Australia; he considers also the implications of *L'Essai sur le don*. Nevertheless he stresses the significance of prestations as symbols of relationship rather than as economic goods.

Lévi-Strauss (1949, p. 606) rightly argues that the structural implications of a marriage can only be understood if we think of it as one item in a whole series of transactions between kin groups. So far, so good. But in none of the examples which he provides in his book does he carry this principle far enough. The reciprocities of kinship obligation are not merely symbols of alliance, they are also economic transactions, political transactions, charters to rights of domicile and land use. No useful picture of 'how a kinship system works' can be provided unless these several aspects or implications of the kinship organization are considered simultaneously. But Lévi-Strauss supposes that there are only 'deux formules d'échange réel' (1949, p. 582). He is concerned simply with whether the alliance is directly reciprocal, group A exchanging women with group B (*échange restreint*), or multiple, several groups exchanging women in a network (*échange généralisé*). Fundamentally he is not really interested in the nature and significance of the counter-prestations that serve as equivalents for women in the systems he is discussing. Because of this limitation of his view he is led to attribute to the Kachin system an instability which it does not in fact possess, and from this point he wanders far afield into wild speculations about the evolutionary history of half the kinship systems of Europe and Asia (1949, pp. 585–90).

Nevertheless, although I consider it quite illegitimate to treat the Kachin system as if it were a fundamental type in a long term historical sequence, I find that a more cautious type of structural comparison leads to very illuminating results.

Some of the societies which Lévi-Strauss himself compares to the Kachin might well repay re-analysis on the lines I have now given, but I will confine myself on this occasion to showing the relevance of my Kachin formulation to two societies which are not considered by Lévi-Strauss at all, namely, the Batak of Sumatra and the Lovedu of South Africa.

The first of these societies is a kind of structural duplicate of that of the Kachin; the second, in a salutary and thought-provoking manner, seems to have much the same kind of structure in reverse.

BATAK[1]

The ethnography of the Batak is very extensive and dates back to the 18th century. Of several published summaries of this work the most compre-

[1] Batak is a collective name for a population of over 1,000,000 residents in the area of Lake Toba in North Central Sumatra. Though the literature divides the Batak into various 'tribes'—Toba, Karo, Timor, etc., the same kinship network seems to prevail throughout. As with the Kachins, however, the 'Batak system' embraces a considerable range of cultural diversity.

hensive is Loeb (1935). Analysis of the literature shows that, if one ignores entirely cultural and demographic factors, the purely structural parallels between Kachin and Batak organization are remarkably close.

The description of Kachin society given in the previous section of this essay was the description of a model; I said nothing about culture or language or population or geography, I was concerned only with the structural interrelations of the systems of kinship, land tenure, economic distribution, social class and political organization. If we analyse Batak society in terms of these same dimensions the pattern that emerges is almost exactly the same. There is no feature of my Kachin model which is not duplicated or closely paralleled in the Batak situation.

The purpose of my Batak analysis is simply to demonstrate that Kachin organization, as described, is in no sense a freak system. My purpose will therefore best be served by listing the Kachin structural characteristics to which I have already referred against the corresponding Batak features.

Kachin	*Batak*[1]
Kinship	
A patriclan system segmented into lineages and sublineages.	ditto (*a*).
The lineage at the local group level is exogamous; the patriclan is not.	ditto (*b*).
The system is idealized as consisting of 5 major clans intermarrying by rule of matrilateral cross-cousin marriage.	ditto, at any rate of the Karo Batak (*c*).

[1] Batak sources:
- (*a*) Loeb (1935, p. 46).
- (*b*) Loeb (1935, p. 47).
- (*c*) Loeb (1935, p. 47).
- (*d*) Fischer (1950); Tideman (1922); Loeb (1935, p. 53).
- (*e*) Loeb (1935, pp. 39–40).
- (*f*) Haar (1948, pp. 206, 208).
- (*g*) Cole (1945, p. 273).
- (*h*) Loeb (1935, pp. 17–38).
- (*i*) Cole (1945, p. 273); Joustra (1911, p. 11).
- (*j*) Loeb (1935, p. 29).
- (*k*) This seems a legitimate inference from Loeb (1935, p. 43).
- (*l*) Warneck (1901, p. 532); Loeb (1935, pp. 58, 42).
- (*m*) Loeb (1935, p. 58).
- (*n*) Loeb (1935, p. 59).
- (*o*) Loeb (1935, p. 59).
- (*p*) Loeb (1935, p. 55).
- (*q*) Loeb (1935, p. 40).
- (*r*) An inference from Fischer (1950) and Warneck (1901, p. 542); Loeb (1935, p. 61).
- (*s*) Loeb (1935, p. 53).
- (*t*) Loeb (1935, p. 39).
- (*u*) Loeb (1935, p. 42).
- (*v*) Warneck (1901).

Kachin   *Batak*

Kinship *(cont.)*

It is in fact the localized lineages   ditto.
which practise this kind of marriage,
and are thereby paired into wife
giving groups (*mayu*)   Batak—*hulahula*.
and wife receiving groups (*dama*).   Batak—*anak boru* (*d*).

Authority

ditto. For 'village' read 'village   '. . . the executive radja of a village
cluster'; for 'district' read 'domain';   is chosen from among members of
for *radja* read *duwa*; for 'sib' read   a certain eligible family. . . . The
'patriclan'; for 'family' read 'local-   family from which the radja is
ized patrilineage', or 'local descent   chosen must be a part of a sib
group'. [It is not the case that all   which is spoken of as the 'ruling
males of the ruling lineage in a   sib.' . . . Among the Karo Batak the
Kachin domain call themselves   five main sibs are to be found in
duwa but all are *du bau amyu*, 'of   every village, although in every
chiefly kind'.]   district a certain one is in the
                                            majority and is generally said to be
                                            the oldest one in the region, as well
                                            as the ruling one. Irrespective of
                                            actual power or following every
                                            male representative of this sib calls
                                            himself radja . . . In some villages
                                            there are more radjas than subjects
                                            (*e*).

Land Tenure

Normal succession rule is ultimo-   Normal succession rule is primogeniture with primogeniture in some   geniture with ultimogeniture in some
areas.   areas (*f*).

The land of the political domain is   ditto. The 'owning' lineage is called
all 'owned' by the lineage of the chief   *namora-mora* ('original') (*g*).
by right of conquest or original
settlement.

The settlement pattern is one of   ditto.
homologous segments.

At the largest extension a domain

Kachin	*Batak*
mung	*urung*
mare	*huta*
kahtawng	*kesain* (*h*).

(*mung*) comprises several village
clusters (*mare*) made up of villages
(*kahtawng*).   ditto (*i*).

Constituent villages (*kahtawng*) are
'owned' by lineages which, locally,
are of inferior status to the chief's
lineage. Those which are not of the
same clan as the chief's lineage are
normally in 'son-in-law' relationship to that lineage.

Kachin	*Batak*
Rent and Brideprice	
Only token rent is paid to the chief in the form of meat from animals killed, work in the chief's field, contributions to the chief's house-building.	ditto (*j*).
The payment of brideprice from *dama* to *mayu* can however be construed as a form of rent.	ditto (*k*).
Apart from objects of symbolic value only, the main part of a brideprice is paid in cattle. Cattle are eventually consumed in prestige feasting. On balance bridewealth cattle tend to move from lower class towards upper class, but as upper class give more and bigger feasts consumption is equalized.	Brideprice is stated to be paid in money. But by a system of pawning or debt-bondage lower class can always borrow from upper class. As these debts are seldom fully redeemed but are cancelled by death, the system is a disguised form of rent refund (*l*).
This orthodox type of marriage is patrilocal.	ditto (*m*).
An alternative, and ill thought of, mode of getting a wife is by labour service. A man works in the household of his future father-in-law for an agreed number of years in lieu of brideprice or at least part of it.	ditto (*n*).
On completion of his service he may, in theory, take his wife back home. In practice he commonly stays on as a tenant of his father-in-law.	In a special form of marriage called *ambil anak*, a man pays no brideprice but lives with his father-in-law and raises heirs to the father-in-law's line. If however he later pays brideprice—even after the death of the father-in-law—the children (or some of them) become his own and he acquires permanent rights in the whole or part of his father-in-law's land (*o*).
Children born to a woman for whom brideprice has not been paid are *n-ji* (bastards). They belong in effect to the woman's group unless legitimized into her lover's line or into her future husband's line as the result of payments.	Position not entirely clear, but seemingly ditto (*p*).

Kachin	*Batak*

Social class

The generally recognized classes of Kachin society apply to lineages rather than individuals. The classes are: Chiefly (*du baw*), aristocratic (*ma gam*), commoner (*darat*) and formerly slaves (*mayam*).	The literature states that there are only three classes—nobles, commoners, slaves. The distinction made between 'ruling family' and 'ruling sib' suggests that there is in fact an additional intermediate class corresponding to Kachin aristocrats (*q*).
Kachin males marry into their own class or into the class above. Kachin females marry into their own class or into the class below.	ditto (*r*).
Thus if there is a difference of class between *mayu* and *dama* it is the *mayu* who rank higher than the *dama*.	ditto. *hulahula* rank higher than *anak boru*. If circumstances result in a *hulahula* group being poorer than Ego's own group, further marriages are avoided and the relationship comes to an end. (*s*).
Practically the differences between social classes are indicated by ownership of prestige symbols and rights over land, rather than any significant difference in economic standards. Chiefs do however sometimes get rich by exploiting their special opportunities as traders. Formerly only the chiefs owned slaves.	ditto (*t*).
Although chiefs gained reputations by having many slaves, there were many economic advantages in being a slave. Bond slavery was a means of obtaining economic credit and political protection from the chief.[1]	ditto (*u*).
Polygyny is rare and a perquisite of the chiefs and aristocrats. It is a device for ensuring continuity of the lineage and the maintenance of political ties rather than an end in itself.	ditto (*v*).

[1] Cf. The Chin *tefa* system described by Stevenson (1943).

It is clear then that in four major institutional fields, namely, those of kinship behaviour, land settlement, social class, and the distribution of consumer goods, the 'model' or structural pattern of Batak society is quite strikingly similar to that of the Kachin. In both societies Kachin type marriage, as manifested in a specific kinship relation between affinally linked lineages, is associated with the same type of 'feudal' land tenure. In both cases the intermarriage of localized lineages of different social class results in a general tendency to transfer economic wealth from the lower class to the upper. In both cases social mechanisms exist whereby this wealth is redistributed and the lower class is not permanently impoverished.

As a model system this total pattern forms an integrated scheme and I cannot regard these correspondences between two such widely separated societies as purely fortuitous.

LOVEDU

The main interest of my second example, as I have already indicated, lies in the fact that, while Lovedu social structure duplicates many of the features which we have encountered among the Kachins and the Batak, the implications of these features sometimes reflect the Kachin pattern in reverse. In particular it appears that when there is a status difference between the 'wife giving' and 'wife receiving' local descent groups, it is the latter and not the former which rank the higher. This of course is also the Chinese pattern, but whereas with the Chinese this order of seniority correlates with a payment of dowry, the Lovedu system involves payment of brideprice. [But see pp. 54–5.] Before discussing this distinction, let me summarize briefly the Lovedu situation.

I will again confine my summary description to factors of a structural kind and will ignore culture, geography and demography. If this summary seems unduly bare, it must be remembered that I am here only concerned to discover the degree to which Kachin type marriage, here associated with a segmentary system of patrilineages and an institution of brideprice, is also correlated with a 'feudal' type political structure, and a hierarchy of social classes.

The Kriges' account (Krige and Krige, 1943, p. 164) of the Lovedu is not presented with this type of analysis in mind. Although they recognize that 'the political system is not a thing apart, standing aloof from marriage and the social structure' they in fact fail to demonstrate how their analysis of the marriage system can be correlated with their analysis of the political system.

The Lovedu are a Southern Bantu tribe resident in north east Transvaal numbering some 33,000 in an area of 150 square miles. The Lovedu proper are an aristocratic section of this population, the remainder being segmented into various sub-tribes of alien origin, but all alike recognize the paramountcy of the Lovedu Queen (Krige and Krige, 1943, pp.

13–14). Lovedu and aliens alike (with certain exceptions) systematically practise Kachin type marriage.

The whole society is organized into a system of patrilineal local descent groups (Krige and Krige, 1943, p. 86). Brideprice is paid in cattle; but these cattle are not consumer goods (Krige, 1939, p. 395).[1] Except in freak situations they are only used to secure a wife for a brother of the bride. Consequently 'ownership of cattle is not the chief or even a very important method of reckoning status. A man will complain, not because he has no cattle, but because he cannot brew beer to maintain his prestige' (Krige and Krige, 1943, p. 42). On the other hand, whereas among the Batak polygyny is something of an abnormality, among the Lovedu it is not only strongly approved of but even, it would seem, a statistical norm.[2]

The objective of marital policy seems to be to build up a village of many huts which has a reputation for giving lavish and frequent beer-drinks. Polygyny is a means to this end.

The Kriges make no direct reference to earlier theoretical discussions of Kachin type marriage but they nevertheless interpret the system as circular. Their ideal model comprises 6 local descent groups marrying in a circle with brides going one way and cattle the other (Krige and Krige, 1943, pp. 66, 145). They recognize that such a model is a simplification of anything that actually occurs and they recognize that the irregularities of actual practice must cause 'social stresses and strains'. But apparently they suppose that these irregularities will cancel out (Krige, 1939, pp. 411ff.). Certainly they seem to have no inkling of Lévi-Strauss's conclusion that, when such systems fail to be circular, class differences will tend to develop. Yet Lovedu is a class stratified society and several of the cases which the Kriges (1939, pp. 413, 416) mention in connection with strained marriage relations concern the marital affairs of village headmen. In each case, it seems, the headman's wife and her brothers start by being of inferior status to the headman himself.

The specific wife giving–wife receiving relationship between two intermarrying local descent groups (Kachin: *mayu-dama*; Batak *hulahula-anak boru*) is for the Lovedu *vamakhulu-vaduhulu*. Between two such groups gift exchanges are continuous. In sum the *vaduhulu* receive women and offerings of beer—often on a very large scale—and in return they contribute cattle and various kinds of assistance including goat meat (Krige and Krige, 1943, pp. 27, 63, 77). The Kriges seem to argue that these exchanges are exact equivalents and tend to stress that the two groups are of equal standing (1943, p. 149). Yet in other contexts they

---

[1] Goats on the other hand are freely slaughtered for consumption as meat.

[2] The Kriges found that 35 per cent of men have more than one wife and that the ratio of married women to married men was 156:100. They argue that the custom of polygyny creates shortages of suitable cross-cousins for the men and that this is the reason why the marriage rule is asymmetrical. The reasoning appears to be invalid (Krige, 1939, pp. 411–12).

stress that a man's cattle-linked sister (i.e., the sister by means of whom a man receives bridewealth cattle to acquire a wife) ranks higher in the social hierarchy than the man himself (1943, p. 101). They also note that a gift of women is the socially recognized mode of offering tribute to a political superior (1943, p. 95) and further that the giving of beer is typically a gesture of honour and an approved form of tribute (1943, pp. 18, 63, 287–8).

My suggestion is that we have here a kind of Kachin structure in reverse. No doubt, as with the Kachins, the majority of marriages are between local descent groups of equal status; but I postulate that, wherever the kin groups are of different status, then there is a very strong tendency for the wife receiving group to rank the higher. Thus a married woman belongs to a higher ranking local group than her cattle-linked brother and receives tokens of honour from his household accordingly. This reversed order of seniority is correlated with the fact that it is the acquisition of extra wives rather than the acquisition of extra cattle that is a major value in Lovedu society.

If this hypothesis be accepted much that is somewhat bizarre and freakish in the Kriges' account becomes structurally meaningful, while at the same time it becomes apparent that there are important gaps in the information which the Kriges provide.

The total political domain of the Lovedu Queen is subdivided into a number of political subdistricts each with its own district head. District headship is, in theory, hereditary though succession is liable to 'manipulation' from the centre. The Queen herself is an anomalous social person, for, though physiologically female, she is sociologically male. Her tributary dependants—i.e., the district heads and 'marginal' foreign chiefs who wish to avail themselves of the Queen's rain magic—pay her tribute in the form of wives (Krige and Krige, 1943, pp. 173–4). From 'foreigners' the Queen accepts these women as gifts without reciprocation; to the district heads of the main Lovedu area she repays the gift with cattle brideprice. As a consequence the Queen is in a sort of master-servant relationship to the 'foreigner' headmen, but in *vaduhulu* (wife receiving) relationship to the district heads.

After a period at Court the 'wives' of the Queen (*vatanoni*) are re-allocated as true wives to other district heads and to Lovedu Court officials of high rank. The new husband pays no brideprice either to the Queen or to the original parents of his bride, but he has an obligation, in due course, to give a daughter of his bride to the Queen as a further *vatanoni* wife. On the other hand, although he has paid no brideprice himself, the new husband is now considered in *vaduhulu* relationship towards the original local descent group of the bride (Krige and Krige, 1943, p. 98).

At first sight there is a striking paradox about this account. Why should the Queen pay out cattle for her wives, but then give the wives away again without getting cattle in return? The purely structural answer seems to be that in this second case the gift is repaid not in cattle but in the person of the woman's daughter. But if we ask why this should be so, the Kriges have no answer. I suggest that the logic of the situation from the Lovedu point of view, is that an inferior does not properly give cattle to a superior. The proper gesture to persons of higher rank is to give women and beer; *vaduhulu* rank above *vamakhulu*.

If this be so then the complicated matter of the Queen's wives makes political sense. This can be seen if we represent the situation by a diagram similar to those already employed in the earlier part of this essay.

In Fig. 14 the lines A, B, C, represent the local descent groups of three headmen A_1, B_1, C_1. C_1 is a 'foreigner' headman; A_1 and B_1 are Lovedu district heads in the sense described above. X is a Lovedu nobleman, a kinsman of the Queen.

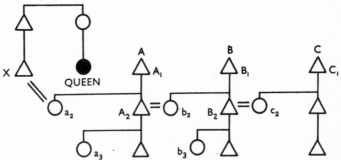

FIG. 14.—Principles of Lovedu political structure
(for explanation see text).

In the first phase of the *vatanoni* procedure, A_1, B_1, C_1 give daughters a_2, b_2, c_2 to the Queen as tribute (*hu lova*). The Queen accepts c_2 simply as tribute; for a_2 and b_2 she pays cattle as brideprice. These three women then spend a period at Court as the Queen's 'wives'. Later they are re-allocated as real wives at the Queen's discretion. We assume that c_2 is given to group B, b_2 to group A, a_2 to the nobleman X. By this action the Queen establishes a hierarchy of precedence, for group B are now *vaduhulu* to group C, group A are *vaduhulu* to group B and X is *vaduhulu* to group A. Moreover the Queen herself is in the status of 'cattle-linked sister' to X (her kinsman). One line of ranking is thus Q—X—A—B—C, Q being the highest. But in addition the Queen is individually the superior of X as 'cattle-linked sister', of A_2 and B_2 as *vaduhulu*, and of C as tribute claiming overlord.

In due course a_3 and b_3 are tendered to the Queen as tribute wives and the process is repeated.

This diagrammatic scheme seems to correspond closely with the actual political hierarchy as described by the Kriges, though in the real pattern there is one further complication.

Among the dependants of the Lovedu Queen there are certain Shangana-Tonga groups whom the Lovedu consider as low caste and with whom marriage is theoretically forbidden. The Queen accepts tribute wives from these groups also. But these women are reallocated to the Lovedu nobility not as wives but as daughters. Then, finally, they are married off to Lovedu commoners. The Kriges do not state whether any cattle are transferred at these marriages and it is not clear whether or not a *vaduhulu/vamakhulu* relationship is extablished thereby but what is evident is that the Shangana-Tonga are thus, by a fiction, kept out of the kinship structure altogether.

This analysis, I think, makes it clear that the intimate and intricate relationship between the hierarchy of rank and the practice of Kachin type marriage—which in the Kriges' account emerges as a kind of paradox since they hold that wife givers and wife receivers should be of equal status—is in fact basic to the whole scheme of political integration and is fully integrated with the total system of values in Lovedu society.

Yet we are left with important elements in the economic structure unexplained. In this scheme the Queen is for ever paying out brideprice cattle but is apparently devoid of any source from which these cattle might be acquired. On this point the Kriges provide us with no information.[1]

THE CONTENT OF PRESTATIONS

What then is the significance of this Lovedu material for our general argument?

It requires, I think, that we re-examine just what is meant by the notion propounded by Granet and Lévi-Strauss that in Kachin type marriage we have a regular exchange of women for 'prestations'. What are these prestations? Lévi-Strauss, though he uses the word, does not, so far as I can discover, examine the nature of this category at all carefully. Yet it has become clear in the course of this essay, that the 'prestations' in a Kachin type marriage system may not only take on a variety of forms, they may have several quite different structural functions.

Consider for example the case of two local descent groups linked in 'wife giving' and 'wife receiving' relationship, and let us assume that one of these is of higher status than the other. Then what are the 'prestations' that pass from one group to the other in the four contexts: Kachin, Batak, Lovedu, Chinese? The answer briefly is given in Table III.

This list is not comprehensive but it illustrates the argument. In any such system of reciprocities one must assume that, overall, both parties—the junior group and the senior group alike—are satisfied with their

---

[1] The only people whom the Kriges (1943, p. 10) mention as giving cattle to the Queen are persons of equal status to the Queen herself—e.g., the former Zulu and Pedi kings.

TABLE III

Variety of 'prestation'	Status of *receiving* group			
	Kachin	*Batak*	*Lovedu*	*Chinese*
a. women	junior	junior	senior	senior
b. labour of men	senior	senior		
of women			senior	senior
c. consumer goods—				
beer	(†)		senior	
meat	senior		junior	
livestock	senior		(*)	
money		senior		(†)
d. non-consumer goods—				
ritual cattle			junior (*)	
jewellery	(†)	?		(†)
ritual objects	(†)			
e. territorial rights	junior	junior	junior	
political protection	junior	junior	junior	junior
f. 'prestige', 'face', 'honour'	senior	senior	senior	senior

* Livestock among the Lovedu must be considered as non-consumable goods
† In these cases similar objects are presented both from senior to junior and *vice versa* according to circumstances.

bargain, and therefore that the exchange account 'balances'. But we cannot predict from first principles how the balance will be achieved because we cannot know how the different categories of 'prestation' will be evaluated in any particular society. A Chinese may be so anxious to secure the patronage of an influential son-in-law that he will pay handsomely for the privilege: a Kachin in the same situation pays to acquire an influential father-in-law. Both are systems of exchange, certainly, but they can only be understood if the categories of just what is exchanged are carefully assessed. In any such analysis it is very important to distinguish between consumable and non-consumable materials; it is also very important to appreciate that quite intangible elements such as 'rights' and 'prestige' form part of the total inventory of 'things' exchanged.

PART 4

Conclusion

What then can be inferred from the theoretical discussions of the first half of this essay and the three brief structural analyses given in the second?

1. A review of the literature has shown that if we ignore various quite hypothetical historical reconstructions the most popular 'explanation' of Kachin type marriage is to see it as the hallmark of an imaginary type of structural system in which 'marriage classes' marry in a circle. Radcliffe-

Brown has shown that this analysis is invalid for the Murngin; I have shown it to be equally invalid for the Kachins.

2. Two major errors are involved in the 'marriage class' argument. The first is to suppose that the groups which are paired as 'wife giving' and 'wife receiving' by the marriage rule are major segments of the society. In fact, in all cases closely examined, they are local descent groups domiciled in the same or closely neighbouring communities. The second error is to suppose that the marriage system in itself constitutes a closed system. In fact, as we have seen, Kachin type marriage is only understandable if it is thought of as one of many possible types of continuing relationship between paired local descent groups.

3. Despite the stimulating quality of Lévi-Strauss's argument, his main proposition is back to front. He argues that the fundamental characteristic of Kachin type marriage is that it is egalitarian—women must be exchanged for goods, on a sort of fixed price equilibrium basis. He perceives that in fact differences of price and differences of status will result, but regards this as the breakdown of the system, and hence as a mechanism in the general process of social evolution. My own argument is almost the reverse of this. As far as the marriage system is concerned, the status relations between group A and group B must be taken as given factors in the situation; a marriage is only one of many possible ways of 'expressing' those relations.

4. When two local descent groups A and B are in relation the 'things' which can be exchanged to express this relationship can be roughly categorized as follows:

I. Tangibles
  (*a*) 'women' and 'men'[1]
  (*b*) labour of men or women
  (*c*) consumer goods and money
  (*d*) capital goods
  (*e*) ritual objects of no intrinsic value

II. Intangibles
  (*f*) 'rights' of a territorial and political nature
  (*g*) relative 'status' or 'prestige'

The last item cannot be defined except in terms of the cultural situation; it is simply 'that kind of reputation which gains a man the admiration of

---

[1] In most of this essay I have referred to the exchange of women in marriage much as if they were chattels. This is of course a gross oversimplification. In most societies the outcome of marriage exchanges is concerned with validating the status of the woman's offspring. In patrilineal societies the husband's group can usually be said to 'buy' the woman's offspring from the wife's group. Yet equally there are cases where the wife's group retain the offspring and 'buy' the sexual services of the husband from the husband's group. This for instance is true of the matrilineal matrilocal Minangkabau and also of the *ambil anak* form of marriage already mentioned.

his fellows', it may be derived from murder in one society, philanthropy in a second, saintliness in a third.

In every relationship between individuals and between groups, items in the above list are exchanged. It is in the nature of most such 'exchanges' that, as regards the tangible items a, b, c, d, e there is always an imbalance on one side or the other. The exchange account is balanced by the intangible items f and g.

If this argument be admitted then the role of women in the total exchange system cannot be discovered from first principles.

It is the error of Hodson, Murdock and the other 'marriage class' enthusiasts to suppose that in a marriage exchange the equivalent of a woman is always another woman. Lévi-Strauss argues that the equivalent of a woman may also be in goods and labour and symbolic objects; but he perceives much less clearly that intangible factors such as rights and reputation can play a part in this exchange without damage to the system. The fact that those Chinese who practise Kachin type marriage pay on balance a dowry and not a brideprice, while their neighbours the Kachins pay a brideprice and not a dowry is a crucial fact of which Lévi-Strauss's theory takes no account.

What can be said on the positive side? I suggest the following minimal propositions which are capable of empirical testing in the field.

1. With Kachin type marriage the relationship between wife giving and wife receiving groups is asymmetrical; hence differentiation of status one way or the other is more likely than not. Such differentiation can be avoided if a small number of neighbouring local descent groups marry in a circle, or if there is a system of balancing rights and obligations—as with the Murngin; but any such system of balances will be unstable.

2. If the status between wife givers and wife receivers is unequal one cannot predict from first principles which of the two groups will be the senior. It seems probable however that in any one cultural situation the position will be consistent. One would not expect that all wife givers are ranked high in one village, and all wife receivers ranked high in the next.

3. The status relations between wife givers and wife receivers must conform to the status relations implicit in other (non-kinship) institutions: e.g., where wife givers are socially superior to wife receivers, one can predict that the political and territorial rights of wife givers will be superior to those of wife receivers, etc.—and *vice versa*. In other words, where Kachin type marriage occurs, it is part of the *political* structure.

4. It seems probable that a costly brideprice *in terms of consumer goods and labour* implies that wife givers rank higher than wife receivers. Conversely a dowry *expressed in consumer goods* implies that wife givers rank lower than wife receivers. A substantial brideprice consisting of objects of symbolic and ritual value only probably goes with high rank and equality of status. The absence of either work payment, brideprice or dowry suggests a breakup of the Kachin type marriage institution.

5. It is a notable characteristic of all the societies considered—Murngin, Kachin, Batak, Lovedu—that the usual characteristics of a tribal organization are lacking. The network of kinship relations embraces a great number of local groups and ties them into a kind of loosely knit political system; but throughout the population so linked there is no strong sense of social solidarity and in some cases there are even wide differences of language and culture between different parts of the one system.

It seems probable that this is a characteristic that may normally be expected to be associated with Kachin type marriage systems, since the asymmetrical relationship between wife givers and wife receivers tends always to push the ramifications of the system to wider and wider limits. The whole structure, in fact, does bear close resemblance to the feudal organization of medieval Europe, which in the same way drew a number of culturally divergent communities into a single political system, though admittedly the integration of that system was, at best, extremely weak.

I certainly do not hold, as Lévi-Strauss seems to do, that the origin of feudal structures is to be found in the breakdown of Kachin type marriage systems; but it does appear to be the case that Kachin type marriage systems correlate very well with political structures of a somewhat feudal type.

This series of hypothetical correlations with Kachin type marriage appears to fit at all the cases examined in this essay and also, so far as the ethnography permits one to judge, those other Kachin type societies such as the Gilyak, the Lakher and the Old Kuki which have been commented upon by Lévi-Strauss; moreover it does so without straining the facts to fit a world embracing theory of social evolution—which can hardly be said of some of Lévi-Strauss's arguments.

In the more general field I suggest that the concept of local descent group developed at the beginning of this essay may have important analytical implications in many cases where the pure descent concept 'lineage' lacks precision. Moreover the arguments which have here been propounded regarding the relevance of status concepts to the analysis of brideprice and dowry have relevance also outside the immediate context of Kachin type marriage.

Finally there emerges from this discussion an important principle of method. If anthropologists are to arrive at any valid principles of social organization, the general method must be comparative. But the original comparative method, exemplified in its most overwhelming form by the work of Frazer, rested on the comparison of cultural traits. Under the impact of functionalism, which insisted upon the analysis of whole cultural systems, this type of comparative method fell into disrepute simply because it appeared to be an impossibility—the body of data that would be involved in an adequate comparison was altogether too vast.

Since 1930, however, Radcliffe-Brown and his followers have had some success in applying a different kind of comparison, namely, that of whole

H

political systems. In a comparative method of this latter kind cultural features are to a large extent ignored, and the 'things' which are compared are really simplified models of the societies under discussion, as observed from a particular point of view. In practice 'the particular point of view' has been that of kinship, and despite the very great value of works such as *Social Organization of Australian Tribes*, *Social Anthropology of North American Tribes*, *African Political Systems* the generalizations that emerge are liable to be distorted on this account.

My own argument, in which to a great extent I follow Lévi-Strauss, is that the comparison of models rather than of 'whole cultures' is a necessary and valid method—indeed I would go much further in such abstraction than has usually been the case with the followers of Radcliffe-Brown. But at the same time I would insist that the comparison must always take into account the whole range of institutional dimensions with which the anthropologist normally has to deal and must start from a concrete reality —a local group of people—rather than from an abstract reality—such as the concept of lineage or the notion of kinship system.

The content of this essay should make it clear why I hold this view. It also provides an excellent illustration of how very misleading comparisons based on the analysis of the kinship dimension alone are liable to be.

4

Polyandry, Inheritance and the Definition of Marriage: with particular reference to Sinhalese customary law

INTRODUCTORY NOTE

As is indicated in the opening paragraph, this paper originated as a commentary upon a lecture by Prince Peter published in the same issue of *Man* and its theme is the simple one that marriage is (to borrow Maine's phrase) 'a bundle of rights'; hence all universal definitions of marriage are vain. Gough (1959) has sought to repudiate this view.

Since the original publication of this paper Dumont has published important material relative to the general theory of South Indian marriage (Dumont, 1957a and b) and parts of a paper by Yalman (1960, 94–99) are also very relevant.

* * * * *

Although polyandry has been an important topic of anthropological discussion for almost a century the definition of the concept remains strikingly unsatisfactory.[1] This is sufficiently indicated by the fact that Fischer (1952) maintains that adelphic polyandry, regarded as a form of polygamy, is non-existent, while H.R.H. Prince Peter of Greece and Denmark (1955), ignoring Fischer, continues to discuss adelphic polyandry as a species of polygamy.

At first sight the issue seems a simple one with the logic all on Fischer's side. The *Notes and Queries* (1951) definition of marriage is: 'Marriage is a union between a man and a woman such that children born to the woman are recognized legitimate offspring of both partners'. Now certainly, in many cases of polyandry, the legal status of the children is similar to that described by Caesar for the ancient Britons (Fischer, 1952, p. 114): 'Wives are shared between groups of ten or twelve men, especially between brothers and between fathers and sons; but the offspring of these unions are counted as the children of those to whom the maid was conducted first.' This clearly is not a condition of polygamy; the children have only one legal father and the woman has only one legal husband. The other

[1] This paper is based in part upon fieldwork carried out in Ceylon in 1954 with the aid of a Leverhulme Research Award and a grant from the Wenner-Gren Foundation.

'husbands' have tolerated sexual access to the woman, but she is not married to them in terms of the *Notes and Queries* definition. The situation is one of plural mating, or, as Fischer would call it, 'polykoity'.

More specifically, Fischer argues that we should reserve the concept of polygamy for situations in which the polygamous spouse goes through a succession of marriage rites with different partners. In adelphic polyandry 'the woman does not contract different successive marriages. There is no reason for this, since the social position of her children is guaranteed completely by the fact that she is married' (Fischer, 1952, p. 114).

Fischer agrees that an institution of polyandrous polygamy is a possibility. For example a woman might be mated to several men in such a way that each of them in turn assumed the role of social father in respect to her successive children. This very approximately seems to be the state of affairs among the Todas, and Fischer concedes that it 'approaches very closely to that of polygamy'. The institution of secondary marriage as described by Smith (1953) is also polyandrous polygamy in Fischer's sense. In both these cases every child has one, and only one, clearly defined social father.

But is it really so certain that the role of social father cannot be vested simultaneously in several different individuals? Is it not possible that in some societies social fatherhood is not an attribute of individuals at all but of a collective corporation which may include several brothers or even fathers and sons?

When Radcliffe-Brown (1941) argued that adelphic polyandry is to be 'interpreted in the light of the structural principle of the solidarity of the sibling group', he presumably had in mind that social fatherhood might sometimes be vested in a collective corporation of this kind, and Prince Peter sought to demonstrate that this is in fact the case. Does this mean that the notion of group marriage is once again respectable?

There is certainly one well attested case of 'corporate polyandry' of this kind, namely that of the Iravas (Aiyappan, 1945, pp. 98–103). Although Aiyappan states that on the occasion of a marriage 'the common practice is for the eldest brother alone to go to the bride's house to fetch her', it is plain, from the further details that he gives, that the eldest brother is here acting as representative of the group of brothers considered as a corporation. Even so, it is not entirely clear what rights this corporation possesses. It is Aiyappan's thesis that *all* marital rights are completely merged in the corporation—that the sexual rights of the individual husbands and the property rights of the individual children are alike indistinguishable. Nevertheless one would welcome more detailed evidence on these points.

There is another way of looking at the problem. Instead of arguing pedantically about whether adelphic polyandry does or does not constitute plural marriage, let us consider whether a definition of marriage solely in terms of legitimacy (*Notes and Queries*, p. 111; Fischer, p. 108) is altogether adequate. There are other definitions of marriage with respectable backing, e.g. 'a physical, legal, and moral union between a man and a woman in complete community of life for the establishment of a family' (Ranasinha, 1950, p. 192). Is the *Notes and Queries* definition any less question-begging than this? What, for example, does the phrase 'legitimate offspring' really connote?

Prince Peter, in the lecture under discussion, seemed to assume that, of the various forms of heterosexual mating recognized and tolerated in any society, there is always one which may properly be described as 'marriage' in the anthropological sense. Yet if we adhere rigidly to our *Notes and Queries* definition this is not the case.

Thus traditionally among the matrilineal Nayar of South India (Gough, 1952 and 1955) a woman had a ritual husband in her *enangar* lineage and also various 'recognized lovers' (*sambandham*), who lacked ritual status; but all of these men were excluded from any legal rights in respect to the woman's children. There was here then no marriage in the strict sense of the term but only a 'relationship of perpetual affinity' between linked lineages (Gough, 1955). The woman's children, however they might be begotten, were simply recruits to the woman's own matrilineage.

Yet as Gough has shown, even in this system, certain *elements* of a normal marriage institution are present.

The notion of fatherhood is lacking. The child uses a term of address meaning 'lord' or 'leader' towards *all* its mother's lovers, but the use of this term does not carry with it any connotation of paternity, either legal or biological. On the other hand the notion of affinity is present, as evidenced by the fact that a woman must observe pollution at her ritual husband's death (Gough, 1955).

Both Gough (1952) and Prince Peter have described the Nayar as having a system of polyandrous marriage. I do not wish to insist that this is a misnomer, but we need to be clear that *if* we agree that the Nayar practise polyandrous marriage then we are using the term 'marriage' in a sense different from that employed by Fischer and by *Notes and Queries*.

My personal view is that the *Notes and Queries* definition of marriage is too limited and that it is desirable to include under the category 'marriage' several distinguishable sub-types of institution.

The institutions commonly classed as marriage are concerned with the allocation of a number of distinguishable classes of rights. In particular a marriage may serve:

A. To establish the legal father of a woman's children.
B. To establish the legal mother of a man's children.
C. To give the husband a monopoly in the wife's sexuality.[1]

---

[1] I use the term 'monopoly' advisedly. I consider that this right *C* is to be regarded as a monopoly control over the disposal of the wife's sexuality rather than an exclusive right to the use thereof. In discussing adelphic polyandry this distinction is important.

D. To give the wife a monopoly in the husband's sexuality.

E. To give the husband partial or monopolistic rights to the wife's domestic and other labour services.

F. To give the wife partial or monopolistic rights to the husband's labour services.

G. To give the husband partial or total rights over property belonging or potentially accruing to the wife.

H. To give the wife partial or total rights over property belonging or potentially accruing to the husband.

I. To establish a joint fund of property—a partnership—for the benefit of the children of the marriage.

J. To establish a socially significant 'relationship of affinity' between the husband and his wife's brothers.

One might perhaps considerably extend this list, but the point I would make is that in no single society can marriage serve to establish all these types of right simultaneously; nor is there any one of these rights which is invariably established by marriage in every known society. We need to recognize then that the institutions commonly described as marriage do not all have the same legal and social concomitants.

If we attempt a typology of marriage on these lines it is at once obvious that the nature of the marriage institution is partially correlated with principles of descent and rules of residence. Thus in a society structured into patrilineal patrilocal lineages we commonly find that right A is far and away the most important element, whereas among the matrilineal matrilocal Nayar, as we have seen, right J is the only marriage characteristic that is present at all. Or again, in the matrilineal virilocal structure of the Trobriands, right G assumes prior, though not altogether unique, importance in the form of *urigubu* (Malinowski, 1932a, pp. 69–75).

Although the early writers on polyandry (e.g. McLennan, 1865) supposed that it was an institution closely associated with matriliny, Prince Peter has pointed out that the best-established cases of adelphic polyandry occur in societies which express patrilineal ideals. This was true of the Kandyan Sinhalese (D'Oyly, 1929); it is true of the patrilineal Iravas of Madras (Aiyappan, 1945) and of the Tibetans (Bell, 1928, p. 88). But it is also the case that the patriliny in these societies is of an ambiguous and rather uncertain type. The position in each case is that while the people concerned profess a preference for patrilocal marriage and the inheritance of landed property through males only, matrilocal marriage and inheritance through females is not at all uncommon (Aiyappan, 1945; Li An-Che, 1947; D'Oyly, 1929, p. 110). Moreover although women who marry patrilocally surrender their claims on their own ancestral land, they receive a dowry of movable goods in lieu.

This aspect of adelphic polyandry, namely that it is intimately associated with an institution of dowry, has previously received inadequate attention. In patrilineal systems of the more extreme type *all* significant property rights are vested in males so that, from the inheritance point of view, marriage does no more than establish the rights of a woman's sons in her husband's property (right *A* above). Fission of the patrimonial inheritance group does of course occur, and when it occurs it is very likely that individual marriages will be cited (retrospectively) as a justification for such a split; the model given by Fortes (1945, p. 199) is typical in this respect. Yet, in such cases, marriage, as such, does not create an independent partible estate.

But when property in land and saleable valuables is vested in women as well as in men, a very different state of affairs prevails; for each marriage then establishes a distinct parcel of property rights and the children of any one marriage have, of necessity, a different total inheritance potential from the children of any other marriage.

Systems of inheritance in which both men and women have property endowment are very general in Southern India, Ceylon and throughout South-East Asia. Such systems are found in association with patrilineal, matrilineal and cognatic descent structures. The general pattern is that the nuclear family, as a unit, possesses three categories of property, namely the entailed inheritance of the father, the entailed inheritance of the mother, and the 'acquired property'—that is, the property owned jointly by the parents by virtue of their operations as a business partnership during the period of the marriage. The children of the marriage are heirs to all three categories of property, but the categories are not merged.

Now it is quite obvious that an inheritance principle whereby women as well as men can be endowed with property conflicts with the ideal that landed property should be maintained intact in the hands of the male heirs. Yet it is a fact that there are many societies which manage to maintain both principles simultaneously. There are a variety of customary behaviours which can best be understood if they are regarded as partial solutions to the dilemma that arises from maintaining these contradictory ideals.

Let us be clear what the dilemma is. On the one hand there is the ideal that the patrimonial inheritance ought to be maintained intact. Full brothers and the sons of full brothers *ought* to remain together in the ancestral home and work the ancestral land. On the other hand, since the wives of these men, when they join the household, bring with them property which will be inherited by their own children but not by their husbands' nephews and nieces, each new marriage creates a separate block of property interests which is in conflict with the ideal of maintaining the economic solidarity of male siblings.

One way out of the difficulty was that adopted in the Jaffna Tamil code of Thesawalamai (Tambiah, 1954, p. 36): the sons inherited the hereditary property of their father, and the acquired property of both spouses was inherited by the sons and the undowered daughters. The dowries to the daughters were given out of the mother's dowry. Systems of double unilineal descent such as that described by Forde for the Yakö operate in a somewhat comparable way (Forde, 1950, p. 306), though the distinction here is between property passed to men through men (the patrilineal inheritance of land rights) and property passed to men through women (the matrilineal inheritance of movables).

The Moslem preference for patrilineage endogamy likewise resolves the conflict between female rights of inheritance and a patrilineal principle of descent. A declared preference for reciprocal or patrilateral cross-cousin marriage may sometimes have similar implications. Indeed, marriage preferences of this latter type seem to be more or less confined to societies in which a substantial proportion of the inheritance rights are transmitted through women. [Cf. Homans and Schneider (1955).]

Adelphic polyandry, I would suggest, is to be understood as yet another variation on the same theme. If two brothers share one wife so that the only heirs of the brothers are the children born of that wife, then, from an economic point of view, the marriage will tend to cement the solidarity of the sibling pair rather than tear it apart, whereas, if the two brothers have separate wives, their children will have separate economic interests, and maintenance of the patrimonial inheritance in one piece is likely to prove impossible. If the ethnographical evidence is to be believed, polyandrous institutions, where they occur, are deemed highly virtuous and tend to eliminate rather than heighten sexual jealousies (Aiyappan, 1937).

In the lecture under discussion, Prince Peter referred repeatedly to contemporary polyandry among the Kandyan Sinhalese. It seems important that we should be clear what the word 'polyandry' means in this case. Sinhalese law does not recognize the existence of polyandrous marriage and it is not possible for any individual to maintain in a law court that he or she is 'the recognized offspring' of two different fathers, nor can a woman bear 'legitimate offspring' to two different husbands, without an intermediate registration of divorce. Thus, strictly speaking, polyandry in Ceylon is not a variety of marriage, if marriage be narrowly defined. On the other hand it is certainly the case that there are parts of Ceylon where two brothers often share a common domestic household with one 'wife', these arrangements being permanent, amicable and socially respectable.[1]

[1] It is difficult to accept Prince Peter's claim that in the Ratnapura District of Ceylon polyandry is so common as to be the norm. The *Census* (1946, Vol. I, Part 2) includes figures for 'customary marriages' as well as 'registered marriages'. The Census enumerators were required to enter as 'married' anyone who 'claimed to be married according to custom or repute' and there seems no reason why they should have excluded 'polyandrous husbands'. However, in all districts, the overall total of 'married' males is roughly equal to the overall total of 'married' females, which does not suggest that the frequency of polyandry can be numerically significant. For Ceylon as a whole the *Census* gave 389,846 women as 'married by custom' and 843,493 as 'legally married by registration'. While this is evidence that the strict definition of legitimate marriage is unrealistic, it does not follow that the anthropologist must accept the Census enumerators' notions of what constitutes customary marriage.

Polyandrous households of this type contrast rather strikingly with the more normal pattern in which two or more brothers live together in a single compound each with his separate 'wife'. This latter situation is characterized by marked restraint between the brothers and even complete avoidance between a man and his 'sister-in-law'.

The 'wives' in such cases may or may not be married according to Sinhalese law. In a high proportion of cases they are not so married. In law the children of these unions are then illegitimate. The children, however, have birth certificates and these certificates give the name not only of the mother but also of the acknowledged father, a circumstance which provides the child with a potential claim to a share of the heritable property of each of its parents.[1] The child therefore, although not the *legitimate offspring* of both its parents, is nevertheless a *legitimate heir* of both its parents. If then the principle of legitimacy be here defined in terms of property rights rather than descent it seems quite proper that Sinhalese customary unions should be regarded as marriages.

Is it then possible in this case to have a polyandrous *marriage*? Legally, no. Since a birth certificate certainly cannot show more than one father, no child possesses the basis for establishing a legal claim to the property of a polyandrous corporation. All the same, it seems probable that in polyandrous households the children do ordinarily inherit jointly the undivided property of the two fathers and that Sinhalese custom recognizes their right to do so. Provided that we are not too pedantic about what we mean by 'legitimate' it does appear that we are dealing here with something that an anthropologist can properly call polyandrous marriage. Even so the issue is by no means clear-cut.

Aiyappan (1945, p. 103), in commenting on the refusal of an English judge to admit the possibility of a woman being simultaneously married to two brothers at the same time, treats the issue as being simply one of a conflict between English law and customary Irava law. But so far as the Sinhalese are concerned the issue is not so simple.

The classical formulation of the former Sinhalese law regarding polyandry appears in Sawers' *Digest* (see D'Oyly, 1929, p. 129):

Polygamy as well as polyandry is allowed without limitation as to the number of wives or husbands—but the wife cannot take a second associated husband

---

[1] *The Report of the Kandyan Law Commission* (1935, paragraphs 199–210) recommends that all children born of non-registered marriages shall be deemed illegitimate and shall be excluded from any share in the entailed property of the father. The *Report* recognizes that this conflicts with the customary law of the pre-British period which did not restrict entailed (*paraveni*) property to the offspring of formal marriages. Ranasinha (1950, Vol. I, Part 1, p. 192) ignores this *Report* and asserts that the highest authorities have held that 'registration was not essential to the validity of a marriage in Ceylon, and the marriage relation could be presumed on adequate evidence of cohabitation and repute'. Certainly in many parts of Ceylon to-day the children of non-registered 'marriages' are treated as having full inheritance rights in their father's property, but whether this right could now be sustained in a Court of Law I am uncertain.

without the consent of the first—though the husband can take a second wife into the same house as his first wife without her consent. The wife, however, has the power of refusing to admit a second associated husband at the request of her first husband, even should he be the brother of the first. And should the proposed second associated husband not be a brother of the first, the consent of the wife's family to the double connection is required.

It is clear that two separate rights are here distinguished. First, there is the right in the wife's sexuality which marriage serves to vest partly, but not completely, in the person of the first husband. The sexual rights of the other husbands are exercised, not by virtue of the marriage, but through the individual consent of the first husband and the joint wife. On the other hand, the ritual of patrilocal marriage—the essence of which is that a man conducts his bride from her father's house to his own (*Report*, 1935, paragraph 168)—serves to establish a relation of affinity between the wife's family as a whole and the husband's family as a whole. The wife's family have no interest in what sexual arrangements pertain unless it is proposed to extend the rights of sexual access beyond the limits of the husband's sibling group.

It is notable that, in this formulation of Sawers, the rights of the children are not mentioned; the ritual procedures of Sinhalese marriage are not concerned with the rights of the potential children. The marriage rite disposes of the woman's sexuality to her first husband; it also has the effect of making a public pronouncement that the woman has been properly endowered so that she has no further claims on her parental property. The status of children arises from quite a different source.

In Sinhalese customary law it was (and is[1]) the rule that if a man and a woman are publicly known to have cohabited together and the woman bears a child, then the woman has a claim on the man for the support of the child (D'Oyly, 1929, p. 84). In ordinary rural practice, all of a man's acknowledged children are equally his heirs whether or not he has at any time gone through a ritual of marriage with the children's mother. Likewise all of a woman's children have equal claims on her inheritance.

My conclusion is that in the Sinhalese case, and very probably in other analogous cases, we are dealing with two different institutions both of which resemble marriage as ordinarily understood, but which need to be carefully distinguished. Neither institution corresponds precisely to the ideal type of marriage as defined in *Notes and Queries*.

On the one hand we have a formal and legal arrangement, by which, so far as Ceylon is concerned, a woman can only be married to one man at a time. 'Marriage' in this sense establishes a relationship of affinity between the family of the bride and the family of the first husband, and it gives the disposal of the bride's sexuality to the first husband, subject to the bride's personal consent. On the other hand we have another institution of 'marriage', which is entered into quite informally but which

[1] See footnote 1, p. 111.

nevertheless, by virtue of its public recognition, serves to provide the children with claims upon the patrimonial property of the men with whom the woman cohabits and publicly resides. This second form of 'marriage', although it establishes the inheritance rights of the children, does not establish their permanent status as members of a corporate descent group, and Sinhalese children, as they grow up, have wide choice as to where they finally align themselves for the purposes of affiliation.

If we accept this second institution as a form of 'marriage', then polyandry in Ceylon is a form of polygamy. If we confine the term 'marriage' to the first institution, polyandry in Ceylon is a form of polykoity. These niceties of definition are worth making because it is important that anthropologists should distinguish the various classes of right that are involved in marriage institutions.

Of greater importance is my hypothesis that adelphic polyandry is consistently associated with systems in which women as well as men are the bearers of property rights. Polyandry exists in Ceylon because, in a society where both men and women inherit property, polyandrous arrangements serve, both in theory and practice, to reduce the potential hostility between sibling brothers.

5

Aspects of Bridewealth and Marriage Stability among the Kachin and Lakher

INTRODUCTORY NOTE

I HAVE referred to the commentators on this paper in my preface. Fortes (1959b) is intended as a 'rejoinder' to the arguments I present here and the comments by Goody (1959) are equally unfavourable. Chapter 1 of this present book reaffirms my view that in some societies affinal alliance is functionally dissociated from any notion of filiation, and that the payment of economic dues as an expression of such alliance is not to be understood as a disguised form of double unilineal inheritance.

Judging from Professor Fortes's comments some of my remarks at the end of this essay are open to misinterpretation so to avoid further ambiguity I must state emphatically that the terms 'complementary filiation' 'complementary descent' and 'double unilineal descent' are all inappropriate to the societies discussed in this paper and that their use leads to conclusions which are not merely misleading but false.

*   *   *   *   *

Readers of *Man* may recollect an extensive correspondence that took place during 1953 and 1954 under the general heading *Bridewealth and the Stability of Marriage* (*Man*, 1953, 75, 122, 223, 279; 1954, 96, 97, 153). This centred round certain propositions first formulated by Professor Gluckman in a contribution to *African Systems of Kinship and Marriage*. The present paper has some bearing on the matters there discussed. The hypotheses which Professor Gluckman sought to defend are to be found at pp. 190–92 of his original article and seem to be three in number:

(1) Divorce is rare and difficult in societies organized on a system of marked Father Right and frequent and easy to obtain in other types.

(2) The frequency of divorce is an aspect of the durability of marriage as such, which in turn is a function of the kinship structure.

(3) The amount of goods transferred (in bridewealth payments) and the divorce rate tend to be directly associated but both are rooted in the kinship structure. It is rare divorce which allows high marriage payments [not high marriage payment which prevents divorce]. Professor Gluckman's argument is related primarily, though not exclusively, to African

materials. In his view the third hypothesis is quite subsidiary to the other two.

The purpose of this paper is not to controvert Professor Gluckman's thesis but rather to draw attention to certain ambiguities.[1] The first of these is the use of the expression 'marked Father Right'. *Father Right* in anthropology is a translation of the Roman legal concept *Patria Potestas*. As such it is not necessarily associated with patrilineal descent. For example, Garo society is certainly organized on matrilineal principles but authority within the co-resident extended family (*nok*) is vested in the senior husband in the group, the *nokma*. It is he who exercises control over his wife's property and disposes of his daughters in marriage. A man has only marginal influence in the affairs of the households of his married sisters. The Garo, though matrilineal, seem to be a Father Right society. But Professor Gluckman was not using the expression in this way. On the contrary, in his essay 'marked Father Right' appears to be a synonym for some such expression as 'strong patrilinearity'.[2] On this reading, his hypotheses presuppose that the descent structure of any particular society can be given a position on a continuous scale, the markers of which might read: Marked Father Right—Moderate Father Right—Bilateral (cognatic) —Moderate Matriliny—Extreme Matriliny. The general thesis seems to be that as we move along this scale from Marked Father Right towards Extreme Matriliny the probability of frequent and easy divorce increases while the probability of quantitatively large bridewealth payments decreases, the causal factor being the type of descent structure.

My method of testing this hypothesis will be to consider the relevant data from three societies which are culturally very similar. All three of these societies are generally described as patrilineal; but whether all or any of them deserve the label 'Marked Father Right' is a matter of definition. Part of my task is to investigate the meaning of this expression; for clearly, unless we know what this phrase means, the truth or untruth of Professor Gluckman's thesis cannot be verified.

My three societies are: (*i*) The *Gumsa* Kachins of North Burma, particularly those living on the Burma–China frontier east of Bhamo. I shall refer to these as 'Ordinary Jinghpaw'. (*ii*) The Gauri Kachins who

---

[1] Professor Gluckman has kindly read this paper in draft and authorizes me to make the following comments on his behalf. He agrees that the above paragraph contains a fair summary of his original argument but suggests that the reader ought to refer to the original article. In summary of his present views he states: 'I do not think that the kind of bridewealth is simply related to agnatic descent, since it is affected by so many other factors. What I do believe is that it is unusual for there to be a high marriage payment in a system with unstable marriage, and therefore high marriage payments are unusual in non-agnatic systems. I may not have stated this quite clearly in my article, but I think it is clear that this is what I meant.'

[2] Professor Gluckman agrees with this statement and says that in any reformulation of his hypothesis he would avoid the expression 'Father Right'.

are immediate neighbours of the 'Ordinary Jinghpaw', but differ from them slightly in matters of dialect and custom. (*iii*) The Lakher, an Assam tribe who are neighbours to the Haka Chin of Burma, whom they closely resemble in general culture. These last live some hundreds of miles to the south-west of the Kachin groups and are not in direct contact with them. Kachin and Haka Chin culture is however so similar in its general aspects that at least one distinguished anthropologist has confused the two groups (Lévi-Strauss, 1949).

In ethnographical accounts of the Kachins, 'Ordinary Jinghpaw' and Gauri are not usually clearly distinguished but, in fact, Gilhodes (1922) is concerned exclusively with Gauri and Hanson (1913) almost exclusively with 'Ordinary Jinghpaw'. Carrapiett (1929) refers to 'Ordinary Jinghpaw' when citing J. T. O. Barnard and to Gauri when citing P. M. R. Leonard, D. W. Rae and W. Scott. Kawlu Ma Nawng (1942), himself a Gauri, is usually writing about 'Ordinary Jinghpaw', in Chapter XI of his work he is writing about Gauri.

The general pattern of marriage that prevails among the Kachins (Jinghpaw as well as Gauri) has been described by me in previous publications (Leach, 1952; 1945); the Lakher system has been analysed by Parry (1932). Briefly the position is that in all three societies there is high evaluation of class hypogamy, while class hypergamy is deplored. A young man is expected to marry a girl of higher social status than himself, and he must in all events avoid marrying a girl of lower status than himself. If anything, the Lakher stress this evaluation even more strongly than the Kachins. Lakher men can have concubines (*nongthang*) of low class but in marriage proper (*nonghia*) the wife is always expected to be of higher status than her husband, and a man may have to postpone marriage for many years to achieve this end (*op. cit.*, pp. 292, 311, 340). In the long run this discrimination has economic as well as snob value. The amount of a girl's brideprice varies according to the rank status of the patrilineage to which she belongs. If her father, her father's father, and her father's father's father have each in turn married women of higher class than themselves, then the girl may be able to claim a brideprice which is higher than that to which her patrilineage would otherwise be entitled (*op. cit.*, p. 311).

Associated with this pattern of hypogamy is a political structure that in some ways resembles feudalism. The system is reflected in a marriage rule which makes it proper to marry a woman of the category of mother's brother's daughter, while prohibiting marriage with the father's sister's daughter. Typically, a man's father-in-law is also his political overlord. What I have written previously with regard to the Kachin in this matter (Leach, 1951; 1954) is valid also for the Lakher.

All three societies have a patrilineal lineage structure, but, among the Lakher, lineages are not, it would seem, ordinarily of the segmentary type. On this point, however, Parry's material is not very specific. [See also

Leach (1960).] The residence pattern and general ecology seem to be very similar in all three cases.

On the other hand, in the matter of bridewealth and divorce the three groups show some interesting variations.

'Ordinary Jinghpaw' seem to fit Professor Gluckman's hypothesis very well. Though semi-permanent pre-marital liaisons are frequent, there is also a formal religious marriage rite (*num shalai*) and once this has been gone through the only orthodox mode of divorce is for the bride to be exchanged for one of her lineage sisters. The marriage itself is indissoluble (Carrapiett, 1929, pp. 35–37; Kawlu Ma Nawng, 1942, p. 60). The wife's children belong absolutely to the lineage of her husband and there is a system of widow inheritance which possibly deserves the name levirate (*Man*, 1954, 96). Bridewealth transactions in this society are complicated and expensive (Hanson, 1913, p. 185), but these do not reach the elaboration of the Lakher system (Parry, 1932, pp. 311–39).

Lakher, on the other hand, seem to run quite contrary to the theory. There is no religious element in the formal marriage rite (*op. cit.*, p. 299). Divorce is easy and apparently frequent (*op. cit.*, p. 343). Widows may remarry and need not remain with the first husband's lineage (*op. cit.*, p. 295). Yet by ordinary criteria [e.g. succession to names, titles, offices] the Lakher seem to be just as patrilineal as the Kachins. Moreover their bridewealth transactions are not only very expensive but extraordinarily complicated. The husband must not only make a large main payment (*angkia*) to the lineage of his wife, but, once his household is established, he must make a payment (*puma*) of similar scale to the lineage of his wife's mother's brother, part of which (*lokheu*) is then transferred on to the lineage of the mother's brother of the wife's mother's brother.

As I have indicated, Gauri custom is in most respects barely distinguishable from that of the 'Ordinary Jinghpaw' but there are some special features with regard to marriage and divorce in which the Gauri somewhat resemble the Lakher. Gauri divorce is not common but is quite possible. Where a marriage is unsatisfactory the easier procedure (as with the 'Ordinary Jinghpaw') is for the bride's lineage to provide another girl as substitute. But where this is not possible the marriage can be brought to an end simply by returning the brideprice (Gilhodes, 1922, p. 222; Leonard in Carrapiett, 1929, p. 37; Kawlu Ma Nawng, 1942, p. 62).

Again, a Gauri widow is only provisionally at the disposal of her husband's lineage. If the latter do not provide a new husband whom her parents consider suitable then they may take her back (against partial repayment of the brideprice). She is then completely free to marry again (Gilhodes, 1922, p. 227).

In contrast, among the 'Ordinary Jinghpaw', 'when once a woman has completed the ceremony of eating rice from her husband's hand at the evening meal of their wedding day, she becomes his wife for all her life' (Kawlu Ma Nawng, 1942, p. 60) and the husband's kin have an inescapable obligation to support her even after the husband's death.

The Gauri have another striking custom which is relevant. Gauri girls often go through the formal marriage ceremony and then immediately return to their own parents where they remain for a number of years before joining their husbands. While they are at home they do not hesitate to entertain lovers, though the latter risk punishment as adulterers. It is considered most shameful for a Gauri bride to settle down with her husband immediately after marriage (Gilhodes, 1923, pp. 221f.). This, I suggest, is a symbolic gesture which serves to discriminate the fact that while the marriage ceremony has served to transfer to the husband's lineage all offspring of the bride, however begotten, the physical person of the bride herself has not been so transferred. She remains a free and independent member of her own original patrilineage.

Now it is true that 'Ordinary Jinghpaw' brides are also rather prone to making a show of running away from their husbands on the marriage night. It is a gesture of contempt for the low status of the husband's group, and it apparently has the approval of the bride's parents. Nevertheless, in my experience, an 'Ordinary Jinghpaw' bride is always immediately sent back to her husband where she thereupon settles down. Of the ethnographers, only Kawlu Ma Nawng (1942, pp. 60, 62), who is himself a Gauri, seems to claim that 'Ordinary Jinghpaw' and Gauri custom are here virtually the same. I admit that 'Ordinary Jinghpaw' and Gauri custom are very close but the difference that exists is not an accident. 'Ordinary Kachin' marriage transfers both the bride and her offspring to the jural control of the husband's lineage; Gauri marriage transfers the offspring only.

The nature of the marriage ceremony itself and the scale and pattern of the brideprice payments among Gauri and 'Ordinary Jinghpaw' seem to be indistinguishable.

Finally as to politics. In writing previously of the Kachin I have suggested that all Kachin *Gumsa* chiefs (including the Gauri) model themselves on Shan princes and that, of all Kachins, the Gauri chiefs have been the most successful in this respect (Leach, 1954, p. 225). As compared with that of the 'Ordinary Jinghpaw', Gauri society is more clearly class-stratified and the chiefs are more effectively autocratic. From my reading of Parry I should judge that the same is true also of the Lakher.

Is anything to be inferred from these various differences? In terms of Professor Gluckman's original hypotheses it should presumably be the case that the Gauri have 'less marked Father Right' than the 'Ordinary Jinghpaw' and the Lakher 'less marked Father Right' than either; for among the 'Ordinary Jinghpaw' divorce is impossible, among the Gauri divorce is possible but rare, and among the Lakher it is easy and frequent. But how can we measure the degree of Father Right? Is it a question of a father's authority over his sons or over his daughters or over both?

In Professor Gluckman's argument the stress is on the rights in a woman acquired by the patrilineage of the woman's husband as a consequence of marriage. But what has this to do with Father Right? Could we not argue that, if Father Right is a variable at all, then, in a patrilineal society, it is concerned with the degree of permanence with which the patrilineage of birth continues to exercise jural control over all its members throughout their lives. Surely the Father Right of a father who retains considerable control over his daughter's person even after she is married is greater than the Father Right of a father who surrenders all such control to his daughter's husband? Even though Professor Gluckman would now withdraw his use of the expression Father Right the problem still remains. What can we mean if we say that, of two patrilineal societies, one is 'more strongly patrilineal' than the other?

Let us look at our specimen material from this point of view. I suggest that as between the 'Ordinary Jinghpaw' on the one hand and the Lakher (and to some extent the Gauri) on the other, there is *no* difference in the system of descent but that there *is* a significant difference in the nature of the institution of marriage.

With the 'Ordinary Jinghpaw', marriage involves a transfer of the bride from the jural control of her own patrilineage to that of her husband, and this transfer is absolute and final. The husband's lineage acquires by the marriage not only rights in the bride's potential children, but also absolute physical control over the person of the bride herself. The strength of the affinal tie in this case rests on the strength of the sibling relationship between the bride and her original patrilineage. In the case of a quarrel it is this sibling link rather than the marriage link that is presumed to give way. The affinal (*mayu/dama*) relationship between brothers-in-law may become ineffective, but this cannot lead to a divorce.

In this case the bridewealth transactions can correctly be described as a 'brideprice'; ownership of the physical person of the bride and all rights that adhere to her are transferred in exchange for the goods of the marriage payment. In this situation, as Professor Gluckman had predicted, divorce is impossible.

With the Lakher on the other hand marriage is concerned only with the begetting of children and the jural status of these children. The husband's group, whose inferior status is emphasized, can be regarded as 'hiring' the procreative powers of the bride for the purpose of raising children of relatively high status. In this way the husband's lineage acquire permanent rights in the children so produced, but they do *not* acquire permanent rights in the person of the bride. On the contrary, the bride never gives up her effective membership in her own superior patrilineage and she is free to return there whenever she likes. The bride's children belong to the husband's group but not absolutely so; her own patrilineage retains a kind of lien on her children (particularly her daughters) so that when these daughters in due course come to be 'hired out' on marriage her original patrilineage claims half the rent.

I

According to some anthropologists (cf. Brenda Seligman, 1928) we should recognize in this last feature a 'submerged' principle of matrilineal descent, but I find this artificial and unhelpful; Kachins and Lakher alike seem to me to have an exclusively patrilineal 'ideology' with no concepts at all that can usefully be described as those of double unilineal descent. My own interpretation is different. The evidence shows, I suggest, that in the Lakher case, the sibling link between the bride and her own patrilineage is never threatened at all. If the affinal link (*patong/ngazua*) becomes ineffective it is the marriage itself that is allowed to come to an end. This is in contrast to the 'Ordinary Jinghpaw' case where the marriage is deemed unbreakable but the sibling link between the wife and her brothers can become ineffective. My argument is, in fact, an exemplification of Professor Gluckman's second hypothesis as cited in the first paragraph of this paper.

The schematic difference, by which 'Ordinary Jinghpaw' marriage establishes an affinal link between lineages the effectiveness of which depends upon the continued recognition of the sibling relationship, while Lakher marriage establishes an affinal link between lineages the effectiveness of which depends upon the continuation of the marriage itself, is illustrated in Figs. 15 and 16. In both cases the 'affinal tie' established by a new marriage is a potentially fragile element in the continuing social structure; in the 'Ordinary Jinghpaw' case the fragility is located in the sibling link between the bride and her lineage brothers; in the Lakher case the fragility is in the marriage relationship itself.

Now it seems to me arguable that it is in the general nature of kinship that a sibling link is 'intrinsically' more durable than a marriage tie. If so, the large and extended marriage payments of the Lakher (which on Gluckman's thesis are paradoxically associated with easy divorce)[1] may be interpreted as an attempt to consolidate the intrinsic weakness of the *patong/ngazua* relationship (cf. Parry, 1932, p. 343).

It may be observed that the fact that the Lakher and Gauri are more sharply stratified—more class conscious—than the 'Ordinary Jinghpaw', also fits with the pattern I have described. Jinghpaw aristocrats 'sell' their daughters outright; Gauri and Lakher disdain to do so, they merely permit their inferiors to have sexual access conditional on the long continued payment of tribute fees.

This perhaps may seem like the language of a stud farm, but the analogy is appropriate. Lakher notions of class do imply that they think of 'good breed' in humans much as we think of 'good breed' in horses. In both contexts 'good breed' is a valuable commodity and available for hire rather than for sale.

But if my readers accept this analysis, what is left of Professor Gluck-

---

[1] I should stress that Professor Gluckman is well aware of instances, even in the African literature, where high marriage payments go with easy divorce, but in his view these cases are 'unusual' (see p. 115, n. 1).

man's original propositions? If the degree of Father Right is a significant variable in these matters where does one locate the maximum? Among the 'Ordinary Jinghpaw' who give their daughters away, or among the Lakher and Gauri who seemingly never do so? If we are required to hold that the 'Ordinary Jinghpaw' are in some way 'more patrilineal' than the Lakher, what is the basis for this discrimination? My purpose, as I said before, is

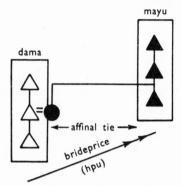

FIG. 15.—'Ordinary Jinghpaw' System.

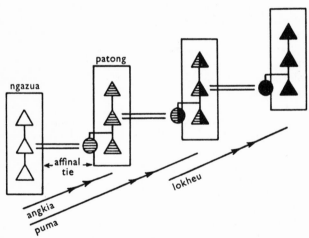

FIG. 16.—Lakher System.

not to controvert Professor Gluckman but rather to seek a clarification of concepts. And this is not just an idle matter of playing with words. It is the whole nature of the concept of 'descent' which is at issue.

Let me elaborate. The importance of the work of Evans-Pritchard and his associates with regard to the general theory of unilinear descent systems is now generally recognized. Since the publication of *The Nuer* (1940) strictly comparable segmentary structures have been reported from many parts of the world (Fortes, 1953). All this has greatly enhanced the general theory of corporate group structure which stems originally from Maine and Weber (Krader, 1956). It has also served to throw great, and perhaps exaggerated, emphasis upon the principle of descent as the fundamental principle of social organization in all relatively 'homogeneous' societies.

In all this analysis the stress has been upon ties within the unilinear corporation or between different corporations linked by ties of common descent. The *structural* ties deriving from marriage between members of different corporations have been largely ignored or else assimilated into the all-important descent concept. Thus Fortes (1953), while recognizing that ties of affinity have comparable importance to ties of descent, disguises the former under his expression 'complementary filiation'. The essence of this concept, which resembles the Roman distinction between agnation and cognation, is that any Ego is related to the kinsmen of his two parents because he is the descendant of both parents and not because his parents were married. The marriage tie itself is of minor importance as compared with the sibling link uniting the 'complementary' parent to his (or her) original descent group. In effect, the structure of affinal relationship is assumed always to be of the type represented by Fig. 15 rather than that shown in Fig. 16. For Fortes, marriage ties, as such, do not form part of the structural system. They are of interest only because they serve to distinguish the individuals from one another. Citing Laura Bohannan he remarks that 'ties . . . arising out of marriage exchanges result in a complex scheme of individuation for distinguishing both sibling groups and persons within the lineage' (Fortes, 1953, p. 33). But the material which I have presented in this paper throws some doubt upon the adequacy of this analysis. For in the Lakher and Kachin cases, although the above generalization is true, it is also the case that the *mayu/dama* and *patong/ngazua* ties are a crucial part of the *continuing* structure of the system. These are systems in which, as usual, 'filiation—by contrast with descent—is bilateral' (*op. cit.*). In the terminology favoured by Fortes and Goody they are patrilineal systems in which the complementary matrilineal descent line assumes very great importance. Ought we then to say that these are systems of double unilineal descent (which conflicts with the ideology of the people themselves as reported by the ethnographers) or should we think again about the relationship between 'corporateness' and 'descent' and qualify our interpretation according to whether the 'complementary filiation' is of the type of Fig. 15 or Fig. 16?

It is relevant here, that, as is indicated in the diagrams, the cross ties linking the different patrilineages laterally are *not* felt by the peoples themselves to be of the nature of descent. The continuity of the structure 'vertically' through time is adequately expressed through the agnatic transmission of a patrilineage name. But the continuity of the structure 'laterally' is not so expressed. Instead, it is maintained by a continuing chain of debt relationships of an economic kind, for it is of the very essence of the *mayu/dama* and *patong/ngazua* ties that some part of the bridewealth payments (*hpu, angkia, puma,* etc.) is left outstanding from generation to generation. It is the existence of these outstanding debts which assert the continuance of the affinal relationship. If the debt is repudiated the affinal tie becomes ineffective; in the 'Ordinary Jinghpaw' case this is likely to lead to feud, in the Lakher case it will lead to divorce and the total cancellation of the affinal (*patong/ngazua*) link.

A similar and related problem exists in the field of Australian studies where there has been a long standing debate as to whether (or in what circumstances) the descent systems described by Radcliffe-Brown and Lloyd Warner can properly be described as systems of double unilinear descent. Schematically this is often the simplest form of description but how far is it adequate? Radcliffe-Brown's attempts to represent the Murngin system as simply a variation of the more usual Australian patterns take cognizance of the kinship structure alone and serve to mask rather than to illuminate the economic elements in the situation. [See pp. 68–72.]

In sum, my problem is this: Are the categories 'complementary filiation' and 'double unilineal descent' as demarcated in Fortes (1953), adequate for the interpretation of data such as I have presented? Or must we, as I suspect myself, take cognizance of the political and economic context before we can give a label to the structural type? I think perhaps that this is the point at which my opinions diverge from those of Professor Gluckman, for at one stage he appeared to be insisting that the kinship structure *per se* is causal to *all* the other factors in the total situation; but perhaps I misunderstood him. The value of the particular instance I have analysed in this paper is that, as between the 'Ordinary Jinghpaw', the Gauri and the Lakher, a very large number of the possibly significant variables are common to all three societies so that it becomes likely that the particular differences that have been noticed are, in fact, the functionally discriminating factors.

I suspect that, in the end, we may have to distinguish two entirely different categories of unilineal descent systems. There is the category into which most of the African lineage systems seem to fall and which would include the non-exogamous lineages of Islamic Western Asia. In this case the ongoing structure is defined by descent alone and marriage serves merely to create 'a complex scheme of individuation' within that structure. In contrast, there is the category of those societies in which unilineal descent is linked with a strongly defined rule of 'preferred marriage'. In this latter case 'complementary filiation' may come to form part of the permanent ongoing structure, but to understand how this comes about we need to consider economic and political factors as well as the kinship structure in isolation.

In both categories of society the principle of unilineal descent is all-important, but it plays an entirely different structural role in the two cases.

6

Two Essays concerning the Symbolic Representation of Time

INTRODUCTORY NOTE

THESE two short essays originally appeared in the Toronto University publication *Explorations*. The amendments which have been made to the text of 'Cronus and Chronos' are largely due to the very helpful suggestions of Mr M. I. Finley of Jesus College, Cambridge.

*   *   *   *   *

I. CRONUS AND CHRONOS

My starting point in this essay is simply *time* as a word in the English language. It is a word which we use in a wide variety of contexts and it has a considerable number of synonyms, yet is oddly difficult to translate. In an English–French dictionary *time* has one of the longest entries in the book; time is *temps*, and *fois*, and *heure*, and *age*, and *siècle*, and *saison* and lots more besides, and none of these are simple equivalents; *temps* perhaps is closest to English *time*, but *beau temps* is not a 'lovely time'!

Outside of Europe this sort of ambiguity is even more marked. For example, the language of the Kachin people of North Burma seems to contain no single word which corresponds at all closely to English *time*; instead there are numerous partial equivalents. For example, in the following expressions the Kachin equivalent of the word *time* would differ in every case:

The *time* by the clock is	....	....	*ahkying*
A long *time*	....	....	*na*
A short *time*	....	....	*tawng*
The present *time*	....	....	*ten*
Spring *time*	....	....	*ta*
The *time* has come	....	....	*hkra*
In the *time* of Queen Victoria	....	....	*lakhtak, aprat*
At any *time* of life	....	....	*asak*

and that certainly does not exhaust the list. I do not think a Kachin would regard these words as in any way synonyms for one another.

This sort of thing suggests an interesting problem which is quite distinct from the purely philosophical issue as to what is the *nature* of

Time. This is: How do we come to have such a verbal category as *time* at all? How does it link up with our everyday experiences?

Of course in our own case, equipped as we are with clocks and radios and astronomical observatories, time is a given factor in our social situation; it is an essential part of our lives which we take for granted. But suppose we had no clocks and no scientific astronomy, how then should we think about time? What obvious attributes would time then seem to possess?

Perhaps it is impossible to answer such a very hypothetical question, and yet, clocks apart, it seems to me that our modern English notion of time embraces at least two different kinds of experience which are logically distinct and even contradictory.

Firstly, there is the notion of repetition. Whenever we think about measuring time we concern ourselves with some kind of metronome; it may be the ticking of a clock or a pulse beat or the recurrence of days or moons or annual seasons, but always there is something which repeats.

Secondly, there is the notion of non-repetition. We are aware that all living things are born, grow old and die, and that this is an irreversible process.

I am inclined to think that all other aspects of time, duration for example or historical sequence, are fairly simple derivatives from these two basic experiences:

(*a*) that certain phenomena of nature repeat themselves

(*b*) that life change is irreversible.

Now our modern sophisticated view tends to throw the emphasis on the second of these aspects of time. 'Time', says Whitehead, 'is sheer succession of epochal durations': it goes on and on (Whitehead, 1927, 158). All the same we need to recognize that this irreversibility of time is psychologically very unpleasant. Indeed, throughout the world, religious dogmas are largely concerned with denying the final 'truth' of this common sense experience.

Religions of course vary greatly in the manner by which they purport to repudiate the 'reality' of death; one of the commonest devices is simply to assert that death and birth are the same thing—that birth follows death, just as death follows birth. This seems to amount to denying the second aspect of time by equating it with the first.

I would go further. It seems to me that if it were not for religion we should not attempt to embrace the two aspects of time under one category at all. Repetitive and non-repetitive events are not, after all, logically the same. We treat them both as aspects of 'one thing', *time*, not because it is rational to do so, but because of religious prejudice. The idea of Time, like the idea of God, is one of those categories which we find necessary because we are social animals rather than because of anything empirical in our objective experience of the world (*Année Sociologique* 5: 248; Hubert and Mauss, 1909).

Or put it this way. In our conventional way of thinking, every interval of time is marked by repetition; it has a beginning and an end which are 'the same thing'—the tick of a clock, sunrise, the new moon, New Year's day . . . but every interval of time is only a section of some larger interval of time which likewise begins and ends in repetition . . . so, if we think in this way, we must end by supposing that 'Time itself' (whatever that is) must repeat itself. Empirically this seems to be the case. People *do* tend to think of time as something which ultimately repeats itself; this applies equally to Australian aborigines, Ancient Greeks, and modern mathematical astronomers (Hoyle, 1950, p. 108). My view is that we think this way not because there is no other possible way of thinking, but because we have a psychological (and hence religious) repugnance to contemplating either the idea of death or the idea of the end of the universe.

I believe this argument may serve to throw some light upon the representation of time in primitive ritual and mythology. We ourselves, in thinking about time, are far too closely tied to the formulations of the astronomers; if we do not refer to time as if it were a coordinate straight line stretching from an infinite past to an infinite future, we describe it as a circle or cycle. These are purely geometrical metaphors, yet there is nothing intrinsically geometrical about time as we actually experience it. Only mathematicians are ordinarily inclined to think of repetition as an aspect of motion in a circle. In a primitive, unsophisticated community the metaphors of repetition are likely to be of a much more homely nature: vomiting, for example, or the oscillations of a weaver's shuttle, or the sequence of agricultural activities, or even the ritual exchanges of a series of interlinked marriages. When we describe such sequences as 'cyclic' we innocently introduce a geometrical notation which may well be entirely absent in the thinking of the people concerned.

Indeed in some primitive societies it would seem that the time process is not experienced as a 'succession of epochal durations' at all; there is no sense of going on and on in the same direction, or round and round the same wheel. On the contrary, time is experienced as something discontinuous, a repetition of repeated reversal, a sequence of oscillations between polar opposites: night and day, winter and summer, drought and flood, age and youth, life and death. In such a scheme the past has no 'depth' to it, all past is equally past; it is simply the opposite of now.

It is religion, not common sense, that persuades men to include such various oppositions under a single category such as *time*. Night and day, life and death are logically similar pairs only in the sense that they are both pairs of contraries. It is religion that identifies them, tricking us into thinking of death as the night time of life and so persuading us that non-repetitive events are really repetitive.

The notion that the time process is an oscillation between opposites— between day and night or between life and death—implies the existence of a third entity—the 'thing' that oscillates, the 'I' that is at one moment in the daylight and at another in the dark, the 'soul' that is at one moment in the living body and at another in the tomb. In this version of animistic thinking the body and the grave are simply alternative temporary residences for the life-essence, the soul. Plato, in the *Phaedo*, actually uses this metaphor explicitly: he refers to the human body as the *tomb* of the soul (psyche). In death the soul goes from this world to the underworld; in birth it comes back from the underworld to this world.

This is of course a very common idea both in primitive and less primitive religious thinking. The point that I want to stress is that this type of animism involves a particular conception of the nature of time and, because of this, the mythology which justifies a belief in reincarnation is also, from another angle, a mythological representation of 'time' itself. In the rest of this essay I shall attempt to illustrate this argument by reference to familiar material from classical Greece.

At first sight it may appear that I am arguing in a circle. I started by asking what sort of concrete real experience lies at the back of our abstract notion of time. All I seem to have done so far is to switch from the oscillations of abstract time to the oscillations of a still more abstract concept, soul. Surely that is worse than ever. For us, perhaps, yes. We can 'see' time on a clock; we cannot see people's souls; for us, souls are more abstract than time. But for the Greeks, who had no clocks, time was a total abstraction, whereas the soul was thought of as a material substance consisting of the marrow of the spine and the head, and forming a sort of concentrated essence of male semen. At death, when the body was placed in the tomb this marrow coagulated into a live snake. In Greek ancestor cults the marked emphasis on snake worship was not a residue of totemism: it was simply that the hero-ancestor in his chthonic form was thought to be an actual snake. So for the Greeks, of the pre-Socratic period anyway, the oscillation of the soul between life and death was quite materially conceived—the soul was either material bone-marrow (in the living body) or it was a material snake (in the tomb) (Onians, 1951; Harrison, 1922).

If then, as I have suggested, the Greeks conceived the oscillations of time by analogy with the oscillations of the soul, they were using a concrete metaphor. Basically it is the metaphor of sexual coitus, of the ebb and flow of the sexual essence between sky and earth (with the rain as semen), between this world and the underworld (with marrow-fat and vegetable seeds as semen), between man and woman. In short, it is the sexual act itself which provides the primary image of time. In the act of copulation the male imparts a bit of his life-soul to the female; in giving birth she yields it forth again. Coitus is here seen as a kind of dying for the male; giving birth as a kind of dying for the female. Odd though this symbolism may appear, it is entirely in accord with the findings of psycho-analysts who have approached the matter from quite a different point of view (Roheim, 1930, pp. 20–26).

All this I suggest throws light upon one of the most puzzling characters in classical Greek mythology, that of Cronus, father of Zeus. [Aristotle] (*de Mundo* Ch. 7) declared that Cronus (Kronos) was a symbolical representation of Chronos, Eternal Time—and it is apparently this association which has provided our venerable Father Time with his scythe (cf. Rose, 1928, p. 69, Note 1). Etymologically, however, there is no close connection between *kronos* and *chronos*, and it seems unlikely that [Aristotle] should have made a bad pun the basis for a major issue of theology, though this seems to be the explanation generally put forward. Whatever may have been the history of the Cronus cult—and of that we know nothing—the fact that at one period Cronus was regarded as a symbol for Time must surely imply that there was something about the mythological character of Cronus which seemed appropriate to that of a personified Time. Yet it is difficult for us to understand this. To us Cronus appears an entirely disreputable character with no obvious temporal affinities.

Let me summarize briefly the stories which relate to him:

1. Cronus, King of the Titans, was the son of Uranus (sky) and Ge (earth). As the children of Uranus were born, Uranus pushed them back again into the body of Ge. Ge to escape this prolonged pregnancy armed Cronus with a sickle with which he castrated his father. The blood from the bleeding phallus fell into the sea and from the foam was born Aphrodite (universal fecundity).

2. Cronus begat children by his sister Rhea. As they were born he swallowed them. When the youngest, Zeus, was born, Rhea deceived Cronus by giving him a (phallic) stone wrapped in a cloth instead of the new-born infant. Cronus swallowed the stone instead of the child. Zeus thus grew up. When Zeus was adult, Cronus vomited up his swallowed children, namely: Hades, Poseidon, Hestia, Hera, Demeter, and also the stone phallus, which last became a cult object at Delphi. Zeus now rebelled against King Cronus and overthrew him; according to one version he castrated him. Placed in restraint, Cronus became nevertheless the beneficient ruler of the Elysian Fields, home of the blessed dead (Frazer, 1915; Roscher, 1884; Nilsson, 1955, pp. 510–517).

3. There had been men when King Cronus ruled but no women; Pandora, the first woman, was created on Zeus' instructions. The age of Cronus was a golden age of bliss and plenty, when the fields yielded harvests without being tilled. Since there were no women, there was no strife! Our present age, the age of Zeus, will one day come to an end, and the reign of Cronus will then be resumed. In that moment men will cease to grow older: they will grow younger. Time will repeat itself in reverse: men will be born from their graves. Women will once more cease to be necessary, and strife will disappear from the world (Hastings, 1908).

4. About the rituals of Cronus we know little. In Athens the most important was the festival known as Kronia. This occurred at harvest time in the first month of the year and seems to have been a sort of New

Year celebration. It resembled in some ways the Roman saturnalia (Greek Cronus and Roman Saturn were later considered identical). Its chief feature seems to have been a ritual reversal of roles—masters waiting on slaves and so on (in general see Nilsson, *op. cit.*).

What is there in all this that makes Cronus an appropriate symbol for Time? The third story certainly contains a theme about time, but how does it relate to the first two stories? Clearly the time that is involved is not time as we ordinarily tend to think of it—an endless continuum from past to future. Cronus's time is an oscillation, a time that flows back and forth, that is born and swallowed and vomited up, an oscillation from father to mother, mother to father and back again.

Some aspects of the story fit well enough with the views of Frazer and Jane Harrison about Corn Spirits and Year Spirits (*eniautos daimon*) (Frazer, *op. cit.*; Harrison, 1912). Cronus, as the divine reaper, cuts the 'seed' from the 'stalk' so that Mother Earth yields up her harvest. Moreover, since harvest is logically the end of a sequence of time, it is understandable enough that, given the notion of time as oscillation, the change over from year's end to year's beginning should be symbolized by a reversal of social roles—at the end point of any kind of oscillation everything goes into reverse. Even so the interpretation in terms of vegetation magic and nature symbolism does not get us very far. Frazer and Jane Harrison count their Corn Spirits and Year Spirits by the dozen and even if Cronus does belong to the general family this does not explain why Cronus rather than any of the others should have been specifically identified as a symbol of Time personified.

My own explanation is of a more structural kind. Fränkel (1955) has shown that early Greek ideas about time underwent considerable development. In Homer *chronos* refers to periods of empty time and is distinguished from periods of activity which are thought of as days (*ephemeros*). By the time of Pindar this verbal distinction had disappeared, but a tendency to think of time as an 'alternation between contraries' active and inactive, good and bad, persisted. It is explicit in Archilochus (seventh century B.C.). In the classical period this idea underwent further development so that in the language of philosophy, time was an oscillation of vitality between two contrasted poles. The argument in Plato's *Phaedo* makes this particularly clear. Given this premise, it follows logically that the 'beginning of time' occurred at that instant when, out of an initial unity, was created not only polar opposition but also the sexual vitality that oscillates between one and the other—not only God and the Virgin but the Holy Spirit as well (cf. Cornford, 1926).

Most commentators on the Cronus myth have noted simply that Cronus separates Sky from Earth, but in the ideology I have been discussing the creation of time involves more than that. Not only must male be distinguished from female but one must postulate a third element, mobile and vital, which oscillates between the two. It seems clear that the Greeks thought of this third element in explicit concrete form as male semen. Rain is the semen of Zeus; fire the semen of Hephaestos; the offerings to the dead (*panspermia*) were baskets of seeds mixed up with phallic emblems (Harrison, 1912, 1922); Hermes the messenger of the gods, who takes the soul to Hades and brings back souls from the dead, is himself simply a phallus and a head and nothing more.

This last symbolic element is one which is found to recur in many mythological systems. The logic of it seems clear. In crude pictorial representation, it is the presence or absence of a phallus which distinguishes male from female, so, if time is represented as a sequence of role reversals, castration stories linked up with the notion of a phallus trickster who switches from side to side of the dichotomy 'make sense'. If Kerenyi and Jung are to be believed there are psychological explanations for the fact that the 'messenger of the gods' should be part clown, part fraud, part isolated phallus (see Radin, 1956, pp. 173–211) but here I am concerned only with a question of symbolic logic. If time be thought of as alternation, then myths about sex reversals are representations of time.

Given this set of metaphors Cronus's myth *does* make him 'the creator of time'. He separates sky from earth but he separates off at the same time the male vital principle which, falling to the sea reverses itself and becomes the female principle of fecundity. The shocking part of the first story, which at first seems an unnecessary gloss, contains, as one might have expected, the really crucial theme. So also in the second story the swallowing and vomiting activities of Cronus serve to create three separate categories—Zeus, the polar opposites of Zeus, and a material phallus. It is no accident that Zeus's twice born siblings are the five deities named, for each is the 'contrary' of Zeus in one of his recognized major aspects: the three females are the three aspects of womanhood, Hestia the maiden, Hera the wife, Demeter the mother; they are the opposites of Zeus in his roles as divine youth (*kouros*), divine husband, divine father and divine son (Dionysus). Hades, lord of the underworld and the dead, is the opposite of Zeus, lord of the bright day and the living; Poseidon, earth shaker, god of the sea (salt water), is the opposite of Zeus, sky shaker (thunderer), god of rain and dew.

The theme of the child which is swallowed (in whole or part) by its father and thereby given second birth, crops up in other parts of Greek mythology—e.g. in the case of Athena and of Dionysus. What is peculiar to the Cronus story is that it serves to establish a mythological image of interrelated contraries, a theme which recurs repeatedly in mature Greek philosophy. The following comes from Cary's translation of the *Phaedo*:

'We have then,' said Socrates, 'sufficiently determined this—that all things are thus produced, contraries from contraries?'

'Certainly.'

'What next? Is there also something of this kind in them, for instance, between all two contraries a mutual twofold production, from one to the other, and from the other back again . . .?' (Cary, 1910, p. 141).

For men who thought in these terms, 'the beginning' would be the creation of contraries, that is to say the creation of male and female not as brother and sister but as husband and wife. My thesis then is that the philosophy of the *Phaedo* is already implicit in the gory details of the myth of Cronus. The myth is a creation myth, not a story of the beginning of the world, but a story of the beginning of time, of the beginning of becoming.

Although the climate may seem unfamiliar, this theme is not without relevance for certain topics of anthropological discussion. There is for instance Radcliffe-Brown's doctrine concerning the identification of alternating generations, whereby grandfather and grandson tend to exhibit 'solidarity' in opposition to the intervening father. Or there is the stress which Lévi-Strauss has placed upon marriage as a symbol of alliance between otherwise opposed groups (Lévi-Strauss, 1945). Such arguments when reduced to their most abstract algebraic form may be represented by a diagram such as this:

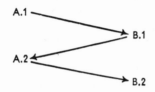

In Radcliffe-Brown's argument the As and the Bs, that are opposed yet linked, are the alternating generations of a lineage; in Lévi-Strauss's, the As and the Bs are the males of contending kir. groups allied by the interchange of women.

My thesis has been that the Greeks tended to conceptualize the time process as a zig-zag of this same type. They associated Cronus with the idea of time because, in a structural sense, his myth represents a separation of A from B and a creation of the initial arrow A——→B, the beginning of life which is also the beginning of death. It is also nicely relevant that Heraclitus should have defined 'a generation' as a period of thirty years, this being calculated 'as the interval between the procreation of a son by his father and the procreation of a son's son by the son', the interval, that is A.1——→B.1——→A.2 (Fränkel, 1955, pp. 251–2).

I don't want to suggest that all primitive peoples necessarily think about time in this way, but certainly some do. The Kachins whom I mentioned earlier have a word *majan*, which, literally, ought to mean 'woman affair'. They use it in three main contexts to mean (*a*) warfare, (*b*) a love-song, and (*c*) the weft threads of a loom. This seems to us an odd concatenation yet I fancy the Greeks would have understood it very well. Penelope sits at her loom, the shuttle goes back and forth, back and forth, love and war, love and war; and what does she weave? You can guess without looking up your *Odyssey*—a *shroud* of course, the time of Everyman. 'Tis love that makes the world go round; but women are the root of all evil. (Onians *op. cit.* refs. to *kairos*. The Greek Ares god of war was paramour of Aphrodite goddess of love.)

II. TIME AND FALSE NOSES

Briefly my puzzle is this. All over the world men mark out their calendars by means of festivals. We ourselves start each week with a Sunday and each year with a fancy dress party. Comparable divisions in other calendars are marked by comparable behaviours. The varieties of behaviour involved are rather limited yet curiously contradictory. People dress up in uniform, or in funny clothes; they eat special food, or they fast; they behave in a solemn restrained manner, or they indulge in licence.

Rites de passage, which mark the individual's social development—rituals of birth, puberty, marriage, death—are often similar. Here too we find special dress (smart uniform or farcical make-believe), special food (feast or fast), special behaviour (sobriety or license). Now why?

Why should we demarcate time in this way? Why should it seem appropriate to wear top hats at funerals, and false noses on birthdays and New Year's Eve?

Frazer explained such behaviours by treating them as survivals of primitive magic. Frazer may be right, but he is inadequate. It is not good enough to explain a world-wide phenomenon in terms of particular, localized, archaic beliefs.

The oddest thing about time is surely that we have such a concept at all. We experience time, but not with our senses. We don't see it, or touch it, or smell it, or taste it, or hear it. How then? In three ways:

Firstly we recognize repetition. Drops of water falling from the roof; they are not all the same drop, but different. Yet to recognize them as being different we must first distinguish, and hence define, time-intervals. Time-intervals, durations, always begin and end with 'the same thing', a pulse beat, a clock strike, New Year's Day.

Secondly we recognize aging, entropy. All living things are born, grow old and die. Aging is the irreversible fate of us all. But aging and interval are surely two quite different kinds of experience? I think we lump these two experiences together and describe them both by one name, time, because we would like to believe that in some mystical way birth and death are really the same thing.

Our third experience of time concerns the rate at which time passes. This is tricky. There is good evidence that the biological individual ages at a pace that is ever slowing down in relation to the sequence of stellar time. The feeling that most of us have that the first ten years of childhood 'lasted much longer' than the hectic decade 40–50 is no illusion. Biological processes, such as wound healing, operate much faster (in terms of stellar time) during childhood than in old age. But since our sensations are geared to our biological processes rather than to the stars, time's chariot appears to proceed at ever increasing speed. This irregular flow of biological time is not merely a phenomenon of personal intuition; it is observable in the organic world all around us. Plant growth is much faster at the beginning than at the end of the life cycle; the ripening of the grain and the sprouting of the sown grain proceed at quite different rates of development.

Such facts show us that the regularity of time is not an intrinsic part of nature; it is a man made notion which we have projected into our environment for our own particular purposes. Most primitive peoples can have no feeling that the stars in their courses provide a fixed chronometer by which to measure all the affairs of life. On the contrary it is the year's round itself, the annual sequence of economic activities, which provides the measure of time. In such a system, since biological time is erratic, the stars may appear distinctly temperamental. The logic of astrology is not one of extreme fatalism, but rather that you can never be quite sure what the stars are going to get up to next.

But if there is nothing in the principle of the thing, or in the nature of our experience, to suggest that time must necessarily flow past at constant speed, we are not required to think of time as a constant flow at all. Why shouldn't time slow down and stop occasionally, or even go into reverse?

I agree that in a strictly scientific sense it is silly to pretend that death and birth are the same thing, yet without question many religious dogmas purport to maintain precisely that. Moreover, the make-believe that birth follows death is not confined to beliefs about the hereafter, it comes out also in the pattern of religious ritual itself. It appears not only in *rites de passage* (where the symbolism is often quite obvious) but also in a high proportion of sacrificial rites of a sacramental character. The generalizations first propounded by Hubert and Mauss and Van Gennep have an extraordinarily widespread validity; the rite as a whole falls into sections, a symbolic death, a period of ritual seclusion, a symbolic rebirth.

Now *rites de passage*, which are concerned with demarcating the stages in the human life cycle, must clearly be linked with some kind of representation or conceptualization of time. But the only picture of time that could make this death-birth identification logically plausible is a pendulum type concept. All sorts of pictorial metaphors have been produced for representing time. They range from Heraclitus's river to Pythagoras's harmonic spheres. You can think of time as going on and on, or you can think of it as going round and round. All I am saying is that in fact quite a lot of people think of it as going back and forth.

With a pendulum view of time, the sequence of things is discontinuous; time is a succession of alternations and full stops. Intervals are distinguished, not as the sequential markings on a tape measure, but as repeated opposites, tick-tock tick-tock. And surely our most elementary experiences of time flow are precisely of this kind: day-night day-night; hot-cold hot-cold; wet-dry wet-dry? Despite the word *pendulum*, this kind of metaphor is not sophisticated; the essence of the matter is not the pendulum but the alternation. I would maintain that the notion that time is a 'discontinuity of repeated contrasts' is probably the most elementary and primitive of all ways of regarding time.

All this is orthodox Durkheimian sociology. For people who do not possess calendars of the Nautical Almanac type, the year's progress is marked by a succession of festivals. Each festival represents, for the true Durkheimian, a temporary shift from the Normal-Profane order of existence into the Abnormal-Sacred order and back again. The total flow of time then has a pattern which might be represented by such a diagram as this (Fig. 17):

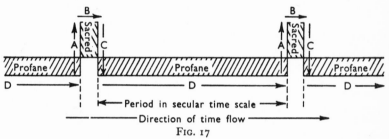

FIG. 17

Such a flow of time is man made. It is ordered in this way by the Societies (the 'moral persons' to use Durkheimian terminology) which participate in the festal rites. The rites themselves, especially sacrificial rites, are techniques for changing the status of the moral person from profane to sacred, or from sacred to profane. Viewed in this Durkheimian way, the total sequence embraces four distinct phases or 'states of the moral person'.

Phase A. The rite of sacralization, or separation. The moral person is transferred from the Secular-Profane world to the Sacred world; he 'dies'.

Phase B. The marginal state. The moral person is in a sacred condition, a kind of suspended animation. Ordinary social time has stopped.

Phase C. The rite of desacralization, or aggregation. The moral person is brought back from the Sacred to the Profane world; he is 'reborn', secular time starts anew.

Phase D. This is the phase of normal secular life, the interval between successive festivals.

So much for Durkheim, but where do the funny hats come in? Well, let me draw your attention to three features in the foregoing theoretical argument.

Firstly let me emphasize that, among the various functions which the holding of festivals may fulfil, one very important function is the ordering of time. The interval between two successive festivals of the same type is a 'period', usually a named period, e.g. 'week', 'year'. Without the festivals, such periods would not exist, and all order would go out of social life. We talk of measuring time, as if time were a concrete thing waiting to be measured; but in fact we *create time* by creating intervals in social life. Until we have done this there is no time to be measured.

Secondly, don't forget that, just as secular periods begin and end in festivals, so also the festivals themselves have their ends and their beginnings. If we are to appreciate how neatly festivity serves to order time, we must consider the system as a whole, not just individual festivals. Notice for example how the 40 days between Carnival (Shrove Tuesday) and Easter is balanced off by the 40 days between Easter and Ascension, or how New Year's Eve falls precisely midway between Christmas Eve and Twelfth Night. Historians may tell you that such balanced intervals as these are pure accidents, but is history really so ingenious?

And thirdly there is the matter of false noses, or to be more academic, role reversal. If we accept the Durkheimian analysis of the structure of ritual which I have outlined above, then it follows that the rituals of Phase A and the rituals of Phase C ought, in some sense, to be the reverse of one another. Similarly, according to the diagram, Phase B ought somehow to be the logical opposite to Phase D. But Phase D, remember, is merely ordinary secular life. In that case a logically appropriate ritual behaviour for Phase B would be to play normal life back to front.

Now if we look at the general types of behaviour that we actually encounter on ritual occasions we may readily distinguish three seemingly contradictory species. On the one hand there are behaviours in which formality is increased; men adopt formal uniform, differences of status are precisely demarcated by dress and etiquette, moral rules are rigorously and ostentatiously obeyed. An English Sunday, the church ceremony at an English wedding, the Coronation Procession, University Degree taking ceremonials are examples of the sort of thing I mean.

In direct contrast we find celebrations of the Fancy Dress Party type, masquerades, revels. Here the individual, instead of emphasizing his social personality and his official status, seeks to disguise it. The world goes in a mask, the formal rules of orthodox life are forgotten.

And finally, in a few relatively rare instances, we find an extreme form of revelry in which the participants play-act at being precisely the opposite to what they really are; men act as women, women as men, Kings as beggars, servants as masters, acolytes as Bishops. In such situations of true orgy, normal social life is played in reverse, with all manner of sins such as incest, adultery, transvestitism, sacrilege, and *lèse-majesté* treated as the natural order of the day.

Let us call these three types of ritual behaviour (1) formality, (2) masquerade, (3) role reversal. Although they are conceptually distinct as species of behaviour, they are in practice closely associated. A rite

K

which starts with formality (e.g. a wedding) is likely to end in masquerade; a rite which starts with masquerade (e.g. New Year's Eve; Carnival) is likely to end in formality. In these puritanical days explicit role reversal is not common in our own society but it is common enough in the ethnographic literature and in accounts of Mediaeval Europe. You will find such behaviours associated with funerals, or with *rites de passage* (symbolic funerals) or with the year's end (e.g. in Europe: Saturnalia and the Feast of Fools).

My thesis is then that *formality* and *masquerade*, taken together, form a pair of contrasted opposites and correspond, in terms of my diagram, to the contrast between Phase A and Phase C. *Role reversal* on the other hand corresponds to Phase B. It is symbolic of a complete transfer from the secular to the sacred; normal time has stopped, sacred time is played in reverse, death is converted into birth. This Good King Wenceslas symbolism is something which has a world wide distribution because it makes logical sense independently of any particular folklorish traditions or any particular magical beliefs.

References

AIYAPPAN, A., 1934. 'Cross-Cousin and Uncle-Niece Marriages in South India'. *Congr. int. Sci. anthrop. ethn.* London.
— 1937. 'Polyandry and Sexual Jealousy'. *Man,* **130.**
— 1945. *Iravas and Culture Change, Bull. Madras Govt. Mus.* N.S. General Section, Vol. V. No. 1.
ANDERSON, J., 1876. *Mandalay to Momein.* London.
(ARISTOTLE), *de Mundo,* (Chapter 7).
BELL, SIR CHARLES, 1928. *The People of Tibet.* Oxford.
BERNDT, C., 1955. 'Murngin (Wulamba) Social Organisation'. *Amer. Anthrop.* **57.**
— 1957. 'In reply to Radcliff-Brown on Australian Local Organisation'. *Amer. Anthrop.* **59.**
BOHANNAN, L. and P., 1953. *The Tiv of Central Nigeria.* London.
BOSE, J. K., 1934a. 'Social Organisation of the Aimol Kukis'. *J. Dep. Letters,* **25.** Calcutta.
— 1934b. 'Dual Organisation in Assam'. *J. Dep. Letters,* **25.** Calcutta.
— 1936. 'The Nokrom System of the Garos of Assam'. *Man,* **37.**
— 1937a. 'Origin of Tri-clan and Marriage Classes in Assam'. *Man,* **37.**
— 1937b. 'Marriage Classes among the Chirus of Assam'. *Man* **37.**
BROWN, G. GORDON and BARNETT, J. H., 1942. 'Social Organisation and Social Structure'. *Amer. Anthrop.,* Vol. XL, pp. 30–36.
CAMERON, A. A., 1911. 'A Note on the Palaungs of the Kodaung Hill Tracts of the Momeik State'. 'BURMA', *Census of India,* Vol. IX, pt. 1, App. A.
CARNAP, R., 1958. *Introduction to Symbolic Logic and its Applications.* New York.
CARRAPIETT, W. J. S., 1929. *The Kachin Tribes of Burma.* Rangoon.
CARY, H., 1910. *Phaedo* translated by Henry Cary in *Five Dialogues of Plato bearing on Poetic Inspiration.* Everyman's Library. London.
Census of Ceylon, 1946. Vol. I, Part 2, *Statistical Digest.* Colombo.
CHATTOPADHAYA, K. P., 1931. 'Contact of Peoples Affecting Marriage Rules'. *Pres. Add. anthrop. Sec. Indian Sci. Congr.*
COLE, F. C., 1945. *Peoples of Malaysia.* New York.
CORNFORD, F. M., 1926. 'Mystery Religions and Pre-Socratic Philosophy'. *Cam. Hist. Magazine,* Vol. 14.
DAS, T. C., 1935. 'Kinship and Social Organisation of the Purum Kukis of Manipur'. *J. Dep. Letters,* **28.** Calcutta.
— 1945. *The Purums.* Calcutta.
DEACON, A. B., 1927. 'The Regulation of Marriage in Ambryn'. *J. Roy. Anthrop. Inst.* **57.**
D'OYLY, JOHN, 1929. *A Sketch of the Constitution of the Kandyan Kingdom (Ceylon).* Colombo.

DUMONT, L., 1957a. *Une Sous-Caste de l'Inde du Sud*. Paris.
— 1957b. 'Hierarchy and Marriage Alliance in South Indian Kinship'. *Occ. Papers, J. Roy. Anthrop. Inst.*
ELKIN, A. P., 1933. 'Marriage and Descent in Eastern Arnhem Land'. *Oceania*, 3.
— 1953. 'Murngin Kinship Re-examined'. *Amer. Anthrop.* 55.
ELKIN, A. P. and BERNDT, C. and R., 1950. *Art in Arnhem Land*. Melbourne and Chicago.
— 1951. 'Social Organisation in Arnhem Land'. *Man*, 51, 249.
EVANS-PRITCHARD, E. E., 1940. *The Nuer*. Oxford.
— 1945. 'Some Aspects of Marriage and the Family among the Nuer'. *Rhodes-Livingstone Papers No. 11*.
FEI, H. T., 1939. *Peasant Life in China*. London.
FIRTH, R., 1936. *We, the Tikopia*. London.
— 1951a. Review of Fortes, M. *The Web of Kinship among the Tallensi* in *Africa*, 21, 155–9.
— 1951b. Review of Elkin and Berndt *Art in Arnhem Land* in *Man*, 51, 76.
— 1955. *The Fate of the Soul* (The Frazer Lecture for 1951). Cambridge.
— 1959. 'Problem and Assumption in the Anthropological Study of Religion'. *J. Roy. Anthrop. Inst.* 89.
FISCHER, H. TH., 1935. 'De Aanverwantschap bij eenige volken van de Nederlands-Indische Archipel'. *Mensch en Maatschappij*, 11.
— 1936. 'Het asymmetrisch cross-cousin huwelijk in Nederlands Indie'. *Tijds., Indisch. Taal-, Land-, Volenk*, 76.
— 1950. 'The Concept of Incest in Sumatra'. *Amer. Anthrop.* 52.
— 1952. 'Polyandry'. *Int. Arch. Ethnog*. Vol. XLVI. No. 1.
FORDE, DARYLL, 1950. 'Double Descent among the Yakö'. *African Systems of Kinship and Marriage*, (eds. Radcliffe-Brown and Forde). Oxford.
FORTES, M., 1945. *The Dynamics of Clanship among the Tallensi*. London.
— 1949. 'Time and Social Structure: an Ashanti Case Study'. *Social Structure* (ed. Fortes).
— 1950. 'Kinship and Marriage among the Ashanti'. *African Systems of Kinship and Marriage*, (eds. Radcliffe-Brown and Forde). Oxford.
— 1953. 'The Structure of Unilineal Descent Groups'. *Amer. Anthrop.* Vol. LV.
— 1959a. *Oedipus and Job in West African Religion*. Cambridge.
— 1959b. 'Descent, Filiation and Affinity: a Rejoinder to Dr Leach'. *Man*, 59.
FORTUNE, R. F., 1933. 'A Note on Some Forms of Kinship Structure'. *Oceania*, 4.
FRÄNKEL, H., 1955. *Wege und Formen Früh-Griechischen Denkens*. Munich.
FRAZER, SIR J. G., 1915. *The Golden Bough* 3rd edn. London.
— 1918. *Folklore in the Old Testament*. London.
FREEDMAN, M., 1958. *Lineage Organisation in Southeastern China*. London.
GEORGE, E. C. J., 1891. 'Memorandum on the Tribes Inhabiting the Kachin Hills', and 'Memorandum on the Kachins of our Frontier'. *Census of India* 'BURMA', Vol. I, App. IV, X.
GIFFORD, E. W., 1916. 'Miwok Moieties'. *Amer. Archaeol. ethn.* 12.
— 1922. 'California Kinship Terminologies'. *Amer. Archaeol. ethn.* 18.

GILHODES, C., 1911. 'Naissance et Enfance chez les Katchins (Birmanie)'. *Anthropos*, Vol. VI, pp. 868–84.

— 1913. 'Marriage et condition de la Femme chez les Katchins (Birmanie)'. *Anthropos*, Vol. VIII, pp. 363–75.

— 1922. *The Kachins : Religion and Customs*. Calcutta.

GLUCKMAN, M., 1950. 'Kinship and Marriage among the Lozi of Northern Rhodesia and the Zulu of Natal' in *African Systems of Kinship and Marriage* (eds. Radcliffe-Brown and Forde). London.

GOODY, J., 1956a. 'A Comparative approach to Incest and Adultery'. *Brit. Jour. Soc.* **7.**

— 1956b. *The Social Organisation of the LoWiili*. London.

— 1959. 'The Mother's Brother and the Sister's Son in West Africa'. *J. Roy. Anthrop. Inst.* **89.**

GOUGH, E. KATHLEEN, 1952. 'Changing Kinship Usages in the Setting of Political and Economic Change among the Nayars of Malabar'. *J. Roy. Anthrop. Inst.* **82.**

— 1955. 'The Traditional Lineage and Kinship Systems of the Nayar'. (Unpublished manuscript in the Haddon Library, Cambridge.)

— 1959. 'The Nayars and the Definition of Marriage'. *J. Roy. Anthrop. Inst.* **89.**

GRANET, M., 1939. 'Catégories matrimoniales et relations de proximité dans la Chine ancienne'. *Ann. Sociol.* Ser B Fasc 1–3.

HAAR, B. TER, 1948. *Adat Law in Indonesia*. New York.

HANSON, O., 1906. *A Dictionary of the Kachin Language*. Rangoon.

— 1913. *The Kachins : their Customs and Traditions*. Rangoon.

HARRISON, JANE, 1912. *Themis*. Cambridge.

— 1922. *Prolegomena to the Study of Greek Religion*. 3rd edn. Cambridge.

HASTINGS, J. (Ed.). 1908. *Encyclopaedia of Religion and Ethics*. Edinburgh. I. 'Ages of the World (Greek and Roman)', pp. 192–200.

HEAD, W. R., 1917. *Handbook of the Haka Chin Customs*. Rangoon.

HERTZ, H. F., 1902. *A Practical Handbook of the Kachin or Chingpaw Language etc.—with an Appendix on Kachin Customs, Laws and Religion*. Rangoon. Photostat reprint Calcutta, 1943.

HILL-TOUT, C., 1907. *British North America*. London.

HOBBES, T., 1957. *Leviathan* (ed. Oakshott). Oxford.

HODSON, T. C., 1921. 'The Garo and Khasi Marriage Systems Contrasted'. *Man in India*, **1.**

— 1922. *The Primitive Culture of India*. London.

— 1925. 'Notes on the Marriage of Cousins in India'. *Man in India*, **5.**

HOMANS, G. C., 1951. *The Human Group*. London.

HOMANS, G. C. and SCHNEIDER, D. M., 1955. *Marriage, Authority and Final Causes*. Chicago.

HOYLE, F., 1950. *The Nature of the Universe*. Cambridge.

HSU, F. L. K., 1940. 'Concerning the Question of Matrimonial Categories and Kinship Relationship in China'. *Tien Hsia Monthly*, **11.** Shanghai.

— 1945. 'Observations on Cross-Cousin Marriage in China'. *Amer. Anthrop.* **47.**

HUBERT, H. and MAUSS, M., 1909. 'Etude sommaire de la représentation du temps dans la religion et la magie'. *Mélanges d'histoire des religions*. Paris.

HUTTON, J. H., 1921a. *Census of India*, **3**. *Assam*. Appendix B.
— 1921b. *The Sema Nagas*. London.
JOSSELIN DE JONG, P. E. DE, 1951. *Minangkabau and Negri Sembilan*. Leiden.
JOSSELIN DE JONG, J. P. B. DE, 1952. *Lévi-Strauss's Theory on Kinship and Marriage*. Leiden.
JOUSTRA, M., 1911. *Batakspiegel*. Leiden.
KAWLU MA NAWNG, 1943. *The History of the Kachins of the Hukawng Valley* (ed. Leyden). Bombay.
KRADER, I., 1956. 'Corporate Groups and the Organisation of Inner Asian Society'. Paper read to Fifth Int. Congr. Anthrop. Ethn. Sci. at Philadelphia.
KRIGE, J. D., 1939. 'The Significance of Cattle Exchanges in Lovedu Social Structure'. *Africa*, **12**.
KRIGE, E. J. and J. D., 1943. *The Realm of the Rain Queen*. Oxford.
KROEBER, A. L., 1938. 'Basic and Secondary Patterns of Social Structure'. *J. Roy. Anthrop. Inst.* **68**, 299–310.
KULP, D. H., 1925. *Country Life in South China : The Sociology of Familism*. Vol. I. New York.
LANG, A., 1887. *Myth, Ritual and Religion*. 2 Vols. London.
LAWRENCE, W. E. and MURDOCK, G. P., 1949. 'Murngin Social Organisation'. *Amer. Anthrop.* **51**.
LEACH, E. R., 1945. 'Jinghpaw Kinship Terminology' (reprinted as Chapter 2 of this book).
— 1951. 'The Structural Implications of Matrilateral Cross-cousin Marriage' (reprinted as Chapter 3 of this book).
— 1954. *Political Systems of Highland Burma* 2nd edn. 1965 London.
— 1957. 'On Asymmetrical Marriage Systems'. *Amer. Anthrop.* Vol. 59, 343.
— 1958. 'Concerning Trobriand Clans and the Kinship Category "Tabu" ' in *The Developmental Cycle of Domestic Groups* (ed. Goody). *Cam. Papers in Soc. Anth.* No. 1. Cambridge.
— 1960. Letter in *Man*. Jan. 1960.
LÉVI-STRAUSS, C., 1945. 'L'Analyse structurale en Linguistique et Anthropologie' *Word*, **1**.
— 1949. *Les Structures élémentaires de la parenté*. Paris.
— 1953. 'Social Structure', in *Anthropology Today* (ed. Kroeber). Chicago.
— 1955. 'The Structural Study of Myth'. *Journ. Amer. Folklore*.
LI AN-CHE, 1947. 'Dege: A Study of Tibetan Population'. *Southw. Journ. Anthrop.* Vol. III. 4.
LOEB, E. M., 1935. 'Sumatra: its History and People'. *Wiener Beitr.* Kulturges Linguistic. **3**.
LOWIE, R. H., 1929. 'Relationship Terms', *Encycl. Brit.*, 14th edn. Vol. XIX.
MABUCHI, T., 1958. 'Two types of Kinship Rituals among Malayo-Polynesian Peoples'. 9th Int. Cong. Inst. Rel. Tokyo.
MCLENNAN, J. F., 1876. *Studies in Ancient History* (First Series—comprising a reprint of *Primitive Marriage* (1865) etc.). London.
MALINOWSKI, B., 1913. *The Family among the Australian Aborigines*. London.

— 1930. 'Parenthood—The Basis of Social Structure' in *The New Generation* (eds. V. F. Calverton and S. D. Schmalhausen). New York.

— 1932a. *The Sexual Life of Savages* (3rd edn.). London.

— 1932b. *Crime and Custom in Savage Society*. London.

— 1935. *Coral Gardens and their Magic*. 2 vols. London.

MAUSS, M., 1923. 'Essai sur le don'. *Ann. Sociol.* N.S. 1.

MEAD, M., 1930. *Social Organisation of Manu'a*. Bishop Museum Bulletin 36. Honolulu.

— 1934. *Kinship in the Admiralty Islands*. *Amer. Mus. Nat. Hist. Anthrop. papers*, 34. New York.

MILLS, J. P., 1926. *The Ao Nagas*. London.

— 1937. *The Rengma Nagas*. London.

MURDOCK, G. P., 1949. *Social Structure*. New York.

NADEL, S. F., 1957. *The Theory of Social Structure*. London.

NAKANE, C., 1958. 'Cross-Cousin Marriage among the Garo of Assam'. *Man*, 58, 2.

NEEDHAM, R., 1958a. 'A Structural Analysis of Purum Society'. *Amer. Anthrop.* 60.

— 1958b. 'The Formal Analysis of Prescriptive Patrilateral Cross-Cousin Marriage'. *Southw. Jour. Anthrop.* Vol. 14.

NILSSON, M. P., 1955. *Geschichte der Griechischen Religion*. (2nd edn.). Vol. 1. München.

Notes and Queries in Anthropology, 1951. Sixth edn. London.

OLDERROGGE, D. A., 1946. 'The Ring Bond between Clans or the Three-Clan Union (Gens Triplex). *Brief Communications* Inst. Ethno. 1. Moscow.

ONIANS, R. B., 1951. *Origins of European Thought*. Cambridge.

PARRY, N. E., 1932. *The Lakhers*. London.

PETER H.R.H. PRINCE OF GREECE AND DENMARK, 1955. 'Polyandry and the Kinship Group'. Lecture to Roy. Anthrop. Inst. summarized in *Man*, 55, 198.

POWELL, H. A., 1956. *Trobriand Social Structure*. Ph.D. Thesis deposited Univ. London.

RADCLIFFE-BROWN, A. R., 1930. 'The Social Organisation of Australian Tribes'. *Oceania*, 1.

— 1940a. 'On Social Structure'. *J. Roy. Anth. Inst.* 70.

— 1940b. Preface to *African Political Systems* (Eds. Fortes, M. and Evans Pritchard, E. E.). London.

— 1941. 'The Study of Kinship Systems'. *J. Roy. Anth. Inst.* 71.

— 1951. 'Murngin Social Organisation'. *Amer. Anthrop.* 53.

— 1953. Letter to Lévi-Strauss cited in Tax, Sol (Ed.) *An Appraisal of Anthropology Today*. Chicago.

— 1957. *A Natural Science of Society*. Chicago.

RADIN, P., 1956. *The Trickster : A Study in American Indian Mythology* (with commentaries by C. G. Jung and Karl Kerényi). London.

RANASINHA, A. G., 1946. *Census of Ceylon*, Vol. 1 Part 1 General report. Colombo, 1950.

RATTRAY, R. S., 1923. *Ashanti*. London.

— 1927. *Religion and Art in Ashanti*. London.

RATTRAY, R. S., 1929. *Ashanti Law and Constitution*. London.

Report of the Kandyan Law Commission, 1935. Sessional Paper XXIV. Colombo.

RICHARDS, A. I., 1950. 'Some Types of Family Structure amongst the Central Bantu'. *African Systems of Kinship and Marriage* (ed. Radcliffe-Brown and Daryll Forde). London.

RICHARDS, F. J., 1914. 'Cross-Cousin Marriage in South India'. *Man*, 14.

RIVERS, W. H. R., 1907. 'The Marriage of Cousins in India'. *J. Roy. asiat. Soc.*

— 1914. *The History of Melanesian Society*. Cambridge.

— 1921. 'Kinship and Marriage in India'. *Man in India*, 1.

ROHEIM, GEZA, 1930. *Animism, Magic and the Divine King*. London.

ROSCHER, W. H., 1884. *Lexikon der Griechischen und Romischen Mythologie*. Leipzig.

ROSE, H. J., 1928. *A Handbook of Greek Mythology*. London.

ROY, R. C., 1936. 'Notes on the Chawte Kuki Clan'. *Man in India*, 16.

RUHEMANN, B., 1948. 'The Relationship Terms of Some Hill Tribes of Burma and Assam'. *Southw. J. Anthrop.* 4.

SALISBURY, R. F., 1956. 'On Asymmetrical Marriage Systems'. *Amer. Anthrop.* 59.

SCOTT, SIR J. G. and HARDIMAN, J. P., 1901. *Gazetteer of Upper Burma and the Shan States*. Pt. 1, 2 Vols. Rangoon.

SELIGMAN, B. Z., 1927. 'Bilateral Descent and the Formation of Marriage Classes'. *J. Roy. anthrop. Inst.* 57.

— 1928. 'Asymmetry in Descent, with Special Reference to Pentecost'. *J. Roy. anthrop. Inst.* 58.

SHARP, LAURISTON, 1934. 'The Social Organisation of the Yir-Yoront Tribe, Cape York Peninsula'. *Oceania*, 4.

SHAW, W., 1928. 'Notes on the Thadou Kukis'. *J.P.A.S.B.* Vol. XXIV.

SMITH, M. G., 1953. 'Secondary Marriage in Northern Nigeria'. *Africa*, Vol. XXIII, 4.

STEVENSON, H. N. C., 1943. *The Economics of the Central Chin Tribes*. Bombay n.d.

TAMBIAH, H. W., 1954. *The Laws and Customs of the Tamils of Ceylon*. Colombo.

TAX, SOL, 1937. 'Some Problems of Social Organisation'. *Social Organisation of North American Tribes, Ch. I* (ed. Eggan). Chicago.

THOMSON, D. F., 1949. *Economic Structure and the Ceremonial Exchange Cycle in Arnhem Land*. Melbourne.

TIDEMAN, J., 1922. *Simeloengoen. Het land der Timoer-Bataks*. Leiden.

VROKLAGE, B. A. G., 1952. 'Die Grossfamiliale und Verwandtschaftsexogamie in Belu, Zentraltimor (Indonesien)'. *Int. Arch. Eth.* Leiden.

WARNECK, F., 1901. 'Das Eherecht bei den Toba-Batak'. *Bijd. Taal-, Land- Volkenke. Nederlandsch Indie*, 53.

WARNER, W. L., 1930–31. 'Morphology and Function of the Australian Murngin type of Kinship'. *Amer. Anthrop.* 32, 33.

— 1937. *A Black Civilisation*. New York.

WEBB, T. T., 1933. 'Tribal Organisation in Eastern Arnhem Land'. *Oceania*, 3.

WEDGWOOD, C., 1929. 'Cousin Marriage'. *Encycl. Brit.* (14th edn.).

WEHRLI, H. J., 1904. 'Beitrag zur Ethnologie der Chingpaw (Kachin) von Ober-Burma'. *Int. Archiv. Ethn. 16 Sup.*

WERDER, P. VON, 1939. 'Staatstypus und Verwandschaftssystem'. *Africa*, Vol. XII.

WESTERMARCK, E., 1921. *The History of Human Marriage.* 5th edn. London.

WHITEHEAD, A. N., 1927. *Science and the Modern World.* Cambridge.

WILSON, M., 1949. *Good Company.* London.

WOUDEN, F. A. E. VAN, 1935. *Sociale Structuurtypen in de Grote Oost.* Leiden.

YALMAN, N., 1960. 'The Flexibility of Caste Principles in a Kandyan Community'. *Aspects of Caste in S.E. India, Ceylon and N.W. Pakistan* (ed. Leach). *Cam. Papers in Soc. Anthrop. No. 2.*

A Select Bibliography of Publications
of E. R. Leach since 1961 bearing on themes discussed in *Rethinking Anthropology*

1961. Asymmetric marriage rules, status difference, and direct reciprocity: comments on an alleged fallacy. *Southwestern Journal of Anthropology*, **17**:343–51.

— Lévi-Strauss in the Garden of Eden: An examination of some recent developments in the analysis of myth. *Transactions of the New York Academy of Sciences*, series 2:**23**:386–96.

1962. On certain unconsidered aspects of double descent systems. *Man*, **62**, 214.

— The determinants of differential cross-cousin marriage (letter). *Man*, **62**, 238.

— Genesis as myth. *Discovery: The Magazine of Scientific Progress*, **23**, 5, 30–5.

— A note on the Mangaian *Kopu* with special reference to the concept of 'Nonunilinear descent' (letter). *American Anthropologist*, **64**:601–4.

1963. 'Did the Wild Veddas have matrilineal clans?' in *Studies in kinship and marriage, dedicated to Brenda Z. Seligman on her 80th birthday*, I. Schapera (ed.), pp. 68–78. Royal Anthropological Institute Occasional Paper No. 16.

— Law as a condition of human freedom. in *The Concept of Freedom in Anthropology*, David Bidney (ed.) Studies in General Anthropology 1.

— The determinants of differential cross-cousin marriage (letters). *Man*, **63**, 87, 228.

1964. 'Comment on Scheffler's note on the Mangaian *Kopu*', *American Anthropologist*, **66**, 427–9.

— 'Anthropological Aspects of Language: Animal Categories and Verbal Abuse' in E. H. Lenneberg (ed.), *New Directions in the Study of Language*. M.I.T. Press.

— 'Telstar et les Aborigènes ou La Pensée Sauvage', in *Annales*. Paris, December.

1965. 'Culture and Social Cohesion', *Daedalus*, Winter 1965. (Later reprinted in Gerald Holton (ed.) *Science and culture*, Houghton Mifflin).

— 'Alliance and Descent among the Lakher: a Reconsideration', *Ethnos* 1963, **2–4**, pp. 237–49.

— 'The Nature of War', *Disarmament and Arms Control*, **3**, pp. 165–83.

— 'Men and Ideas: Frazer and Malinowski', *Encounter*, (Nov.).

— 'Claude Lévi-Strauss—Anthropologist and Philosopher', *New Left Review*, (Nov./Dec.).

February 1966

LONDON SCHOOL OF ECONOMICS
MONOGRAPHS ON SOCIAL ANTHROPOLOGY

Titles marked with an asterisk are now out of print. Those marked with a dagger have been reprinted in paperback editions and are only available in this form.

*1. 2. RAYMOND FIRTH
   The Work of the Gods in Tikopia, 2 vols., 1940. (Revised edition in preparation.)

   *3. E. R. LEACH
   Social and Economic Organization of the Rowanduz Kurds, 1940.

   *4. E. E. EVANS-PRITCHARD
   The Political System of the Anuak of the Anglo-Egyptian Sudan, 1940

   *5. DARYLL FORDE
   Marriage and the Family among the Yakö in South-Eastern Nigeria, 1941.

   *6. M. M. GREEN
   Land Tenure of an Ibo Village in South-Eastern Nigeria, 1941.

   7. ROSEMARY FIRTH
   Housekeeping among Malay Peasants, 1943. 2nd edition revised, 1966.

   *8. A. M. AMMAR
   A Demographic Study of an Egyptian Province (Sharquiya), 1943.

   *9. I. SCHAPERA
   Tribal Legislation among the Tswana of the Bechuanaland Protectorate, 1943. (Revised edition in preparation.)

   *10. W. H. BEKCETT
   Akokoaso: A Survey of a Gold Coast Village, 1944.

   11. I. SCHAPERA
   The Ethnic Composition of Tswana Tribes, 1952.

   *12. JU-K'ANG T'IEN
   The Chinese of Sarawak: A Study of Social Structure, 1953. (Revised edition in preparation.)

   *13. GUTORM GJESSING
   Changing Lapps, 1954

   14. ALAN J. A. ELLIOTT
   Chinese Spirit-Medium Cults in Singapore, 1955

   *15. RAYMOND FIRTH
   Two Studies of Kinship in London, 1956

   16. LUCY MAIR
   Studies in Applied Anthropology, 1957.

   †17. J. M. GULLICK
   Indigenous Political Systems of Western Malaya, 1958.

†18. MAURICE FREEDMAN
Lineage Organization in Southeastern China, 1958.

†19. FREDRICK BARTH
Political Leadership among Swat Pathans, 1959.

*20. L. H. PALMIER
Social Status and Power in Java, 1960.

†21. JUDITH DJAMOUR
Malay Kinship and Marriage in Singapore, 1959.

†22. E. R. LEACH
Rethinking Anthropology, 1961.

23. S. M. SALIM
Marsh Dwellers of the Euphrates Delta, 1962.

†24. S. VAN DER SPRENKEL
Legal Institutions in Manchu China, 1962.

25. CHANDRA JAYAWARDENA
Conflict and Solidarity in a Guianese Plantation, 1963.

26. H. IAN HOGBIN
Kinship and Marriage in a New Guinea Village, 1963.

27. JOAN METGE
A New Maori Migration: Rural and Urban Relations in Northern New Zealand, 1964.

28. RAYMOND FIRTH
Essays on Social Organization and Values, 1964.

29. M. G. SWIFT

3

3   1965.

Dr Leach's brilliant and provoking essays have already been through two impressions in hardback edition. The title essay is an expansion of the first Malinowski Memorial Lecture in which Dr Leach set out to challenge much of the thinking of his fellow anthropologists. Also included is his remarkable logical exercise on Jinghpaw kinship terms, his original comparative study of cross-cousin marriage, and two other articles on marriage and marriage stability, as well as a pair of essays on the symbolic representation of time. The editors have also included in this paperback edition a select bibliography of Dr Leach's important publications from 1959–1966.

Dr Leach is Reader in Social Anthropology in the University of Cambridge and Provost of King's College.

'It is characteristic of Leach that he brings to anthropological problems an exceptional freshness and acuity of mind, producing analyses of genuine originality that deserve the closest study.'

Derek Freeman in *Man*

'There is no-one in England more fitted by temperament and critical finesse for rethinking anthropology than Dr Leach, and in this role he is rendering an essential service to anthropology, particularly to anthropology in Great Britain.'

A. P. Elkin in *Oceania*

DATE DUE

GAYLORD			PRINTED IN U.S.A.